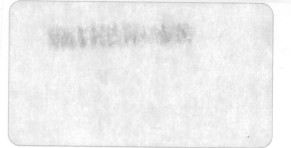

FORBIDDEN LOVE

Español con India.
Mestizo.

Mulato con Española.
Morisco.

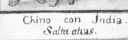

Chino con India.
Salta atras.

Lobo con China
Gibaro.

Español con Mora
Mulato.

FORBIDDEN *Love*

THE SECRET

HISTORY OF

MIXED-RACE

AMERICA

GARY B. NASH

HENRY HOLT AND COMPANY • NEW YORK

Henry Holt and Company, Inc.
Publishers since 1866
115 West 18th Street
New York, New York 10011

Henry Holt is a registered
trademark of Henry Holt and Company, Inc.

Published in Canada by Fitzhenry & Whiteside Ltd.,
195 Allstate Parkway, Markham, Ontario L3R 4T8.

Library of Congress Cataloging-in-Publication Data
Nash, Gary B.
Forbidden love: the secret history of mixed-race America / Gary B. Nash.
p.   cm.—(Edge Books)
Includes bibliographical references and index.
Summary: Presents accounts of how mainly anonymous Americans have
defied the official racial ideology and points out how guardians of
the past have written that side of our history out of the record.
1. Mestizos—United States—History.   2. Mestizos—United States—Biography.
3. United States—Race relations.   [1. Mestizos—Biography.   2. Racially mixed people—
Biography.   3. United States—Race relations.]   I. Title.
E184.M47N47   1998   305.868'72073—dc21   98-12154

ISBN 0-8050-4953-3

First Edition—1999

Printed in the United States of America
on acid-free paper. ∞

1   3   5   7   9   10   8   6   4   2

Book design by Debbie Glasserman

Grateful acknowledgment is made for permission to reprint the following:
The song "You've Got to Be Carefully Taught" was written by Richard Rodgers and
Oscar Hammerstein II. Copyright © 1949 by Richard Rodgers and Oscar Hammerstein II.
Copyright renewed. Williamson Music owner of publication and allied rights throughout
the world. International copyright secured. Reprinted by permission. All rights reserved.
Arna Bontemps wrote the poem "A Black Man Talks of Reaping." Reprinted by the permission
of Harold Ober Associates Incorporated. Copyright 1963 by Arna Bontemps.

Contents

F O R B I D D E N   L O V E

Introduction

"Ah, what a stirring and a seething! Celt and Latin, Slav and Teuton, Greek and Syrian—black and yellow. Yes, East and West, and North and South, the palm and the pine, the pole and the equator, the crescent and the cross—how the great Alchemist melts and fuses them with his purging flame! Here shall they all unite to build the Republic of Man and the Kingdom of God."

Israel Zangwill, "The Melting-Pot" (1908)

This book is about our most enduring problem: race. Racial categories—black, white, Asian, Indian, Latin, Teutonic, Semitic—seem to prove how different one group of human beings is from another. But when you look at the so-called races, the categories crumble. Your race does not come from your genes but from the beliefs of the people around you. Racial classifications are definitions placed on already mixed populations in an effort to give these highly diverse groups essential and binding characteristics. *Forbidden Love* shows how people have tried to separate humanity into such groupings. It shows the harms that racial categorization has caused, how a nation of immigrants from every corner of the earth has wrestled with this problem, and how we have painfully begun to recognize that the only race is the human race.

Two groups have never met without mingling their blood. But then each society has chosen its own way of defining the people in it. Each nation has had its own way because each has had a distinctive beginning and each a unique course of development. The story recounted here, a largely hidden story in our textbooks, shows how Americans built racial classifications and how some Americans have defied the way society defined them and dared to dream of a mixed-race nation. Their lives show that the blending of races is not un-American; it is being American.

This book may upset some people because it does not hesitate to describe a past in which powerful Americans passed laws, spun scientific theories, judged court cases, wrote tracts, created popular entertainment, and preached the belief that every person has one and only one race and that walls must be built to prevent intimacy, love, and marriage between people who supposedly belong to different races. But if this history exposes this difficult past, it also celebrates a long line of rebels and idealists who have defied the racial code devised to keep people apart. *Forbidden Love* is about insistent boundary patrollers and daring boundary crossers.

Readers should be aware at the outset that my use of certain words, such as race, racial, and interracial, is unavoidable despite the fact that the concept of race has almost no basis in science. Once a concept has entered common use, and has been supported by apparently scientific, religious, legal, literary, and popular pronouncements, it becomes part of that nation's history. The idea is real, even if the beliefs are wrong. When many important people come to believe in the concept of "race," and put so much stock in describing, categorizing, and defining races, it is not easy to convince people that there are no biologically defined groups that share essential mental, physical, or cultural characteristics. That is exactly what today's scientists generally agree upon: The racial boxes into which people have been fit—and have fit themselves—lack any objective foundation. The reversal of scientific certitudes cannot easily erase age-old attitudes and behavior that have produced deep cultural, social, economic, and political divisions. Announcing that race is a myth, that it has been socially constructed and historically shaped rather than biologically determined, can only chip away at, but not remove, a powerful legacy.

Yet Americans, and others in the world, have been changing their attitudes and their behavior regarding racial border leaping with great rapidity in recent decades. We read in amazement that before World War II, the Australian government systematically tore the children of European-

Aboriginal marriages away from parents in the belief that placing the children in orphanages was the only hope of salvaging doomed and probably defective children of ill-advised interracial love. We shake our heads at new books describing the sterilization of hundreds of thousands of women not just in Nazi Germany but in the United States, Sweden, Norway, Denmark, Finland, Canada, and Britain in this century in order to protect the racial purity of these nations. We wonder that in our grandparents' day, to skirt laws prohibiting the marriage of white and black partners, a white man would transfer blood from the African-American woman he loved in order to assert that he was black himself. We gape at the absurdity that a woman who was "white" could give birth to a male child who could not marry a woman of the same color as his mother. My students at UCLA are astounded to hear that until 1947 a graduating senior who was Japanese-American could not legally marry a classmate who was "white"; that a graduating senior defined as "Negro" could only marry a person who was also defined as "Negro"; that a Mexican-American graduate could not marry an Asian-American or white American or African-American. As the new millennium approaches, our astonishment at bygone laws and bygone eugenics programs reveals the changes that have occurred in our lifetimes.

In working on this book, I have been assisted enormously by Edith Sparks. Samantha Holtkamp has also helped. Carlos Cortes, David Hollinger, J. Jorge Klor de Alva, and Jeffrey Prager offered shrewd advice on an essay that was the seed from which this book sprouted. Marc Aronson, my editor at Henry Holt and Company, was both astute editor and inspiring discusser of half-formed ideas.

Three young friends served as Generation X readers of the manuscript so that the author could know that he was not writing nonsense. Jessica Barclay-Strobel, Marco Duanti, and Emily Hutters provided a reality check and gave me opportunities to rewrite cloudy passages. I wrote this book with their generation in mind.

FORBIDDEN LOVE

The America That Might Have Been

One dank day in January of 1617 the wealthy crowd in a London theater could hardly pay attention to the performance on stage of Ben Jonson's play *Christmas His Masque*. There sitting next to King James and Queen Anne were the royal couple's special guests: John Rolfe and Pocahontas, man and wife. Rolfe was a dashing adventurer who had just returned from Virginia, the outer edge of the fledgling English empire. Pocahontas, renamed Rebecca by the English, was the beautiful daughter of Powhatan, another king, who ruled over a domain as large and populous as any English county. Pocahontas had already set London atwitter when she appeared at the king's court. Many considered her the most beautiful and well-mannered lady in the land.

AN ANGLO-INDIAN STORY

The marriage of these two very different inhabitants of Virginia was the first recorded interracial union in North American history. How did such a partnership come about? For the first ten years of their settlement on the

Painted at the time she was presented to the court of King James, Pocahontas appears in a red velvet jacket over a dark dress with gold buttons. She holds a fan of three ostrich feathers. We can only imagine how her elaborate shoulder collar of white lace must have felt for a young woman accustomed to loose-fitting, comfortable clothes. [National Portrait Gallery, Smithsonian Institution.]

shores of the Chesapeake Bay, Englishmen seemed very unlikely to have anything to do with Indian women. Most arrived with the fear that Indians would be hostile. When 144 English males clambered off the sailing ships *Susan Constant, Godspeed,* and *Discovery* in the spring of 1607, they expected to fight with native peoples, as other Europeans had done. One of the English leaders, John Smith, wrote that they were surprised when Powhatan, chief of a confederacy of Indian tribes, brought food to the half-starved newcomers. "It pleased God . . . to move the Indians to bring us corn, ere it was half ripe, to refresh us, when we rather expected . . . they would destroy us." In Smith's mind, only a God who favored the English could explain Powhatan's kind gesture.

English suspicions about Powhatan and his people were made worse in

December 1607, when the natives took Smith prisoner. What followed is one of the best known—though least understood—moments in American history. Apparently Powhatan sentenced Smith to die. Yet, at the critical moment, as the warriors prepared to deliver the death blows, Pocahontas, the chief's favorite daughter, threw herself on Smith to save him. About twelve years old at the time, Pocahontas had been a frequent visitor to Jamestown, the fortified main settlement of the English. Undoubtedly she had been sent by her father to act as a bridge between the English and Powhatan's people. The whole execution and rescue had been staged in advance. For Powhatan, this dramatic rescue was a chance to demonstrate his power and his desire to forge a bond with the English. However, Smith and other Virginians (as well as early historians and recent Disney screenwriters) took Pocahontas's gesture as a spontaneous outburst of love for the English. To them this seemed an un-Indian-like act attributable to English superiority or perhaps, once again, to God's intervening hand.

In the aftermath of the incident, Pocahontas became a kind of ambassador from her father to the struggling Jamestown Colony. She soon became fluent in English and kept her father informed on the state of the English settlers. By late 1608, with more colonists arriving in struggling Jamestown, Smith, a veteran soldier and fearless (if reckless) adventurer, became president of the colony's council. He regarded the Indians as sly, treacherous enemies bent on driving the English out of their territory. So he sent his men to burn Indian canoes, fields, and villages in order to extort food supplies. If Smith was determined to defeat Powhatan, the Indian chief was equally determined to drive the intruders back onto their ships. Powhatan called Pocahontas home, and for the next five years the Virginians skirmished with Powhatan's people.

In 1613, when she was seventeen years old, Pocahontas was kidnapped by the English. By luring the chief's favorite daughter aboard a ship, the English hoped to force Powhatan to return his English prisoners and to make him pay a large quantity of Indian corn. While held captive Pocahontas was instructed in the Christian faith by the minister and missionary Alexander Whitaker. Then she met the twenty-nine-year-old widower John Rolfe, a successful tobacco planter. Soon Pocahontas and Rolfe fell in love.

C Smith taketh the King of Pamavnkee prifoner 1608

In England, many readers of John Smith's *Generall Historie of Virginia,* published in 1624, got their first look at Pocahontas's father from this view of Smith seizing the much taller Powhatan by the hair and threatening to club him in 1608. By the time the book reached the public, Pocahontas and John Rolfe were both dead.

Powhatan reluctantly agreed to the first Anglo-Indian marriage in American history. He sent one of her uncles and two of her brothers to solemnize the wedding on April 5, 1614.

In part, Pocahontas's bond with Rolfe was a political arrangement, as were so many royal marriages. But it was also a marriage inspired by love and compassion. In a letter to Virginia's governor, Rolfe revealed the many different feelings he had about making this historic match. He began with strong emotions. "My heart and best thoughts are and have been a long time so entangled and enthralled" with Pocahontas, he wrote, and that he could hardly "unwind" himself from his love for her. Yet fear about marrying an Indian woman made him tremble. He was not "ignorant of the heavy displeasure which almighty God conceived against the sons of Levi and Israel for marrying strange wives," nor of the displeasure of his countrymen that he would suffer if he succumbed to his love for "one whose education hath been rude, her manners barbarous, her generation accursed."

He couldn't banish his love, Rolfe explained to the governor. And it was "not any hungry appetite" for a sexual partner that led him to marry Pocahontas. A man of his status could easily have found an English Christian wife "more pleasing to the eye." But the marriage was "for the good of the plantation, the honor of our country, for the glory of God, for mine own salvation, and for the converting to the true knowledge of God and Jesus Christ an unbelieving creature, namely Pocahontas."

Rolfe's letter shows that his countrymen had strong feelings about marrying women of another society and that their negative view had to do with the Indians' "rude" education, "barbarous" manners, and "accursed" condition. The Europeans saw strange, native people as uncivilized, pagan, and scarcely redeemable. But nowhere in Rolfe's exploration of his feelings and fears do we find any mention of race or skin color. Religion and culture, not race, defined the difference, as Europeans saw it, between "us" and "them." Rolfe hoped the marriage could bring a soul to the Christian church and peace to two warring societies. He also knew it was dangerous, if not blasphemous, to cross this boundary. But he was too "entangled" in feelings to let go.

After a short stay in England, Rolfe and Pocahontas, now with a baby boy, planned to return to Virginia. But Pocahontas suddenly fell ill, and a grief-stricken Rolfe watched his young wife die at age 21 of influenza shortly after boarding ship for the long voyage back to Virginia. With his mixed-race son (whose descendants still live in Virginia) Rolfe reached the Chesapeake Bay, where he married again in 1620. Two years later, Rolfe died in an all-out assault mounted by his uncle-in-law, Opechancanough, a half brother of Pocahontas's father, Powhatan. This attack, inspired by English settlers' violence and land encroachment, resulted in the death of one-third of the tobacco planters. Thereafter, Indian and English intermarriage in Virginia was a rarity.

The union of Rolfe and Pocahontas could have become the beginning of an openly mestizo—or racially intermixed—United States. In the early seventeenth century, negative ideas about "miscegenation"—the marriage of partners from different racial stocks—hardly existed. Indeed the word itself was not invented until 250 years later, when it first appeared in a book fanatically opposed to black-white intermarriage. King James I was not worried about interracial marriage. He fretted only about whether Rolfe, a commoner, was entitled to wed the daughter of a king. Nearly a century later, a wealthy Virginia planter, Robert Beverley, still had no racial compunctions about Indian women. In his *History and Present State of Virginia* (1705), Beverley described Indian women as "generally beautiful, possessing uncommon delicacy of shape and features." He regretted that Rolfe's intermarriage was not followed by many more.

William Byrd, another powerful Virginia planter, commended what he called the "modern policy" of racial intermarriage employed in French Canada and Louisiana. He knew that the French, vastly outnumbered, built alliances and avoided warfare in this way. Byrd confessed his preference for light-skinned women, although his secret diary reveals that skin color rarely curbed his sexual appetite for women of any hue. But he was sure that English "false delicacy" blocked a "prudent alliance" with Indians that might have saved Virginians much tragedy.

Although interracial marriages were rare between white Virginians and Indians, the notion that they might be distasteful was a late development.

Down to the time of the American Revolution, colonial councils saw no reason to ban intermarriage with Native Americans, with only two exceptions—in North Carolina and briefly in Virginia. Nearly two centuries after Virginia's founding, Patrick Henry almost pushed through the state legislature a law offering bounties for white-Indian marriages and free public education for interracial children (which was available to no children at this time). In the third year of his presidency, Thomas Jefferson pleaded "to let our settlements and theirs [the Indians'] meet and blend together, to intermix, and become one people." Six years later, just before returning to Monticello after serving two terms as president, Jefferson promised a group of western Indian chiefs that "you will unite yourselves with us by marriage, your blood will run in our veins, and will spread with us over this great island."

AN AMERICAN STORY

In 1809, almost two centuries after Pocahontas sat in a London theater with James I, sixteen-year-old Sam Houston ran away from his older brothers, who had apprenticed him to a shopkeeper in eastern Tennessee. Houston made his way west ninety miles to Hiwassee Island, where he took up life among the Cherokee, whose women often married Scots traders. Houston was soon adopted by Ooleteka, a Cherokee chief (known by whites as John Jolly). Ooleteka named the lad Kelanu—"The Raven." Showing the rebelliousness he would display all through his life, Houston defied his older brothers when they found him among the Cherokee and wanted to take him back. He told them that he preferred "measuring deer tracks to tape measures—that he liked the wild liberty of the Red men better than the tyranny of his own brothers. . . . So they could go home as soon as they liked."

For three years, until he was nineteen, Houston spoke the Cherokee language, ate Cherokee food, and in effect became a "white Indian." He returned to white society in 1812, but he would never forget his Cherokee experience or his love for those people.

After a brief attempt at teaching school, Houston joined a Tennessee infantry regiment to fight in the War of 1812. Son of a military officer, Houston went off to war with his mother's parting gift, a gold ring inscribed inside with one word: "Honor." The adopted son of the Cherokee soon met up with his old Indian friends in the heat of battle. Under the command of Andrew Jackson, major general of the Tennessee militia, Houston's regiment fought alongside the Cherokee against the Creek allies of the British at the Battle of Horseshoe Bend in March of 1814. His thigh torn by a barbed arrow and with two rifle balls in his right shoulder, Houston performed with extraordinary heroism. His valor helped to carry the day that ended the Creeks' fierce defense of their ancient homelands and the British war against the Americans in the lower South.

After the war, Houston renewed his Cherokee ties. At General Andrew Jackson's request, he went to meet with Ooleteka. His mission was to convince the Cherokees to give up their lands, coveted by the Americans, and follow the first band of their brothers who had moved west of the Mississippi River to the Arkansas Territory. Having labored to arrange the fairest deal possible for his friends, Houston stood beside the Cherokee delegation to Washington in 1818, appearing before President James Monroe in full Indian dress, turbaned and colorfully attired in a hunting shirt.

Only twenty-five years old, Houston had done his best for his Cherokee brothers, but reluctantly he urged them to move west, away from land-hungry whites. Next he began a tumultuous, often violent, roller-coaster ride of a political career. After serving two terms in the U.S. House of Representatives, he won election as governor of Tennessee in 1827 at the age of thirty-four. But he never lost his love for Cherokee life. After a disastrous three-month marriage, he suddenly resigned his governorship of Tennessee and rejoined the Western Cherokee, now living in the Arkansas Territory. When his friend Andrew Jackson heard of Houston's flight to the Cherokee, he exclaimed, "My God, is the man *mad?*" Ooleteka felt otherwise. He welcomed his adopted son warmly. "I have heard that a dark cloud has fallen on the white path you were walking, and when it fell in your way you turned your thoughts to my wigwam. I am glad of it—it was done by the Great Spirit."

Ooleteka, chief of the Western Cherokees, was painted by George Catlin—the most prolific painter of American Indians before the Civil War. One wonders if Ooleteka, known to the Americans as John Jolly, wore such a mixture of Indian and white clothes when his niece married Houston. [Smithsonian Institution.]

The Cherokees granted Houston, soon after he rejoined them, "all the rights, privileges, and immunities of a citizen of the Cherokee Nation . . . as though he was a native Cherokee. . . ." Houston became so thoroughly Cherokee that he dressed like his adopted people, refused to speak English, and "was seen armed only with the bow and arrow with which he had become dexterous when a boy." His first biographer pictured Houston and Chief Ooleteka "seated on the floor . . . feeding each other . . . with the common spoon."

For three years, Houston lived among the Western Cherokee. Twice he made trips to Washington as their unofficial ambassador. Wearing Indian clothing, he negotiated truces among the Osage, Creek, and Cherokee nations. He also lobbied effectively for reform of the Indian Agency system and to safeguard the Arkansas lands that the Cherokee had been guaranteed in their 1818 treaty with the United States government.

While living among the Cherokee, Houston married a part-Indian woman. She was the tall, beautiful Tiana Rogers Gentry. Her thoroughly intermixed family had great prestige and power among the Cherokee in Arkansas. She was the daughter of Captain John Rogers, a prominent white trader to the Cherokees who had himself married a part-Cherokee woman. Her uncles were Ooleteka, Houston's adopted father, and his brother, Chief Tallantuskey, head of the Western Cherokees in this era. Houston had fought alongside many of Tiana Rogers Gentry's brothers and uncles in the Battle of Horseshoe Bend.

Until recently, biographies of Houston omitted this Cherokee marriage, which in any event couldn't outlast Houston's lifelong restlessness, monumental temper, heavy drinking, and oversized ambition. Houston himself admitted that he too often "buried his sorrows in the flowing bowl . . . and gave himself up to the fatal enchantress alcohol." And when the gentle Ooleteka cautioned his adopted son on his heavy drinking, Houston turned on him, attacking him violently. Cherokee warriors pulled Houston off the chief and left him to sober up. When he returned to himself, Houston apologized and begged Ooleteka's forgiveness. But a year later, in 1832, Houston bid farewell to the Cherokees and headed for Texas to fight his way to fame. Although he left his Cherokee wife behind, he took with him his enduring feeling for her people.

Having involved himself with a New York company speculating in Texas land, Houston hatched grand schemes for creating an Anglo-Indian republic in the Mexican Territory of Texas. For Houston, an Anglo-Indian America was not a wild dream. Mixed-blood leaders such as John Ross had already led the Cherokees toward a way of life that blended white and Indian customs. For example, in 1808, the tribe's scattered villages joined together under a National Council of Cherokees, which adopted a written legal code combining elements of both Anglo-Saxon and Indian law. In

Sam Houston made a point of dressing in full Indian regalia on his two trips to Washington as an ambassador for the Cherokee Nation. Through clothing, Houston presented himself as "Indian," in effect announcing his new identity and obliging American political leaders to accept him on Cherokee terms. [San Jacinto Museum.]

1827, the Cherokee created a constitution and established a newspaper, both patterned after those of nearby states. Soon Cherokee families began leaving ancient, communally owned settlements to live in log cabins on private farmsteads. By the 1830s, the Cherokees were the most assimilated Native Americans on the continent. They even adopted the white settlers' practice of owning enslaved Africans.

Houston was one of many frontier Americans in the 1830s who were eager to control Texas. For years, land-hungry Americans had been settling there, pragmatically acknowledging Catholicism as Mexico's official religion, though few practiced it. As their numbers grew, the Americans came to think of Texas as an American domain. Houston, however, envisioned it as an independent nation south of the Red River where many indigenous tribes, along with displaced Cherokees, Creeks, and Choctaws, might find refuge beyond the reach of grasping white frontiersmen.

Houston imagined himself as the governor, president, or emperor of this vast region in which Indian tribes would put aside ancient hostilities and create a peaceful confederation. Cherokees would be foremost among the many tribes. But first, Texas had to be wrested from Mexico. "The morning of glory is dawning upon us," proclaimed Houston in 1835, after being made commander of American troops at Nacogdoches, Texas's second-largest town. Houston's declaration of Texas's independence from Mexico fired the blood of American settlers. For Mexicans, this was an open-and-shut case of landgrab dressed up in high-flown language such as "War in defense of our rights, our oaths, and our constitutions is inevitable in Texas! Our war-cry is 'Liberty or death.' "

Houston had already helped negotiate purchases of land in Texas for thousands of Creeks and Cherokees who were moving south from the Arkansas Territory. His main Cherokee friend in this was Chief Bowles (or "The Bowl"), who had led hundreds of Cherokee families to Texas in 1818. Although it has never been clearly documented, Chief Bowles claimed to have given his daughter in marriage to Houston.

By 1835, Houston's hopes for a racially intermixed Texas had fused with his enormous thirst for land and his hopes that he could lead the Americans in Texas to independence. In 1835, he emerged as a leader of the

Texas rebels. He welcomed war with the Mexicans, but it was not a fight that he relished if Mexico could convince the Indian tribes of Texas—including Houston's Cherokee friends—to side with them. Such an alliance was not unlikely because the Indians were no less vulnerable to American land hunger than were the Mexicans. To prevent this, Houston negotiated a treaty in February of 1836 with Chief Bowles that guaranteed his Cherokee friends a vast tract of Texas land as a permanent home in exchange for their promise that they would not fight along with the Mexicans against the Americans. It was a treaty that guaranteed Indian support for an independent Texas.

After emerging as the conquering hero at San Jacinto, where the Texan rebels defeated the Mexicans in April 1836, Houston was elected president of the now independent Republic of Texas. One of his first actions was to urge the legislature to ratify the treaty with the Cherokees that guaranteed them their new homeland.

Though Houston had worked to protect the Cherokees from white settler racism and violence, his successor as president of the Texas republic, Mirabeau Bonaparte Lamar, adopted a policy of Cherokee expulsion or extinction. In 1839, when the Texas army attacked the Cherokee, Houston's old friend Chief Bowles died holding a sword inscribed to him by Houston. On the battlefield, a Cherokee warrior removed a metal canister that hung from Chief Bowles's neck by a cord. It contained the treaty, drafted and signed by Houston but never ratified by the Texas Senate, guaranteeing the Cherokee lands in Texas forever.

WHAT IS RACE?

Who are we as Americans? What makes us who we are? What are we as individuals and as a nation? To answer these questions we look to our family, our religion, our region, our social background, and our gender, even to which political party we favor.

We also look toward race to define ourselves. For many Americans, race matters most of all. This is so because race has counted greatly in the way our society developed. Race has been a dividing line—separating people, determining where we can live, sanctioning discrimination in employment, dictating who can fight in the nation's wars, and determining who we can marry. Race prejudice, it has been said, is America's fatal flaw, our social Achilles' heel. It has been the awful and gruesome stumbling block confronting every generation since the slave-owning Founding Fathers proposed a set of lofty principles designed to lead this nation forward to freedom, equality, social justice, and peace.

But what is "race," this weighty shaper of history? In terms of science, no such thing as race exists. Though we speak and act as if there were distinctly separate racial groups, there is more genetic variation *within* any grouping that we call a "race" than *between* any two such groups. How can we tell who is "black" in America, when almost all "African-Americans" have European, Native American, and many other ancestors? The absurdity of trying to define races, as we will explore in detail later, reached its pinnacle when state legislatures began defining anyone with "one drop of black blood" as a "Negro." Among the thousands of drops of blood circulating in the human body, how can one drop determine that person's right to live in a neighborhood, drink from a water fountain, ride a bus, or hold a job?

In the nineteenth century, anthropologists poured their intellects and energies into the attempt to classify all the peoples of the world, from the pygmies of Borneo to the Aleuts in Alaska, according to biological distinctions. They examined cranial cavities, measured noses, noted body hair, described lips, and categorized hair and eye color. In the name of science, individuals with advanced degrees from prestigious universities carried out this exacting work in order to define precisely the various physiological types of humankind. Much was at stake in this effort. If physiological characteristics, with skin color prominent among them, could be "scientifically" categorized, it would be possible to rank degrees of "cultural development" on a scale that reached from "savagery" to "civilization."

It should come as no surprise that this massive effort of European and American anthropologists resulted in the "scientific proof" of the superiority of the Caucasian peoples of Europe and North America. But if this "modern" effort to give race theory a scientific basis was Western in origin, it was not an idea confined to the West. Going back to ancient days, people in many parts of the world believed themselves superior to different-looking people they encountered. Around the planet, race theories developed, such as in India, where a color-coded caste system rested on the idea of inherently inferior types of people; and in China, where subjected people were regarded as subhuman; and in Arab lands, where dark-skinned Africans below the Sahara were enslaved and often held in contempt.

Today, genetic sciences have wiped away this long effort to establish a hierarchy of human types. Biology no longer recognizes race as a meaningful category. While genes do determine individual physical traits, those traits do not add up to a set of abilities or disabilities associated with a "race." The rules of race are invented and reinvented by human beings to suit their own preconceptions. Over time, they become so established that we believe they are "real" and "scientific." Yet there is no objective evidence to support classifying a person as belonging to one "race" or another, or to say that there is a set number of distinct races. Europeans fashioned different vocabularies and codes of race relations based upon their own needs and upon ideas concerning how "lesser" people should be classified, treated, and separated. For example, "Negro" came to have different meanings in Brazil than it had in the United States, and those meanings were not based upon genetic difference but rather reflected different local conditions and beliefs. A person's "race" can change merely by going to a new place that has different racial categories. As one of today's most eminent anthropologists reminds us, "The 'reality' of race is thus as much a social as a biological reality." This social reality is highly arbitrary—down to the present day, when, for example, the U.S. Census Bureau is only beginning to accept that Americans can have a mixed racial inheritance. This system is breaking down because people are refusing to identify themselves according to past definitions and are rebelling against the use of race as a device for allocating privileges.

If the system of racial sorting is now breaking down, when did it build up? Quite recently in the long course of human activity, it turns out. If John Rolfe and Pocahontas had lived long enough, they might have been surprised to read about the theory of Georges-Louis Leclerc de Buffon (1707–1788), one of eighteenth-century Europe's leading authorities on natural history. Buffon held that the pale skin of Europeans represented the "real and natural color" of the human race. Anyone not pale-skinned, he theorized, had undergone a change in skin color and facial structure brought about by climate, diet, or even social custom. Buffon and those who followed his ideas came to believe in a racial constellation that equated "whiteness" with physical purity. All non-white peoples, they suggested, had been altered from the original and natural human state.

Not all Europeans accepted this emerging racial hierarchy in which lighter was more natural and darker more unnatural. Johann Friedrich Blumenbach (1752–1840) poked fun at the absurdity of such a self-serving view of the world. "If toads could speak," he wrote, they would doubtless rank themselves as "the loveliest creature upon God's earth."

Buffon's theory took hold because Europeans, for several centuries, had been journeying beyond their own countries and encountering various peoples who looked very different from themselves. Whether Portuguese, Spanish, French, English, or Dutch, they needed a way to make sense of these strangers. Race became a way for Europeans to differentiate themselves from the "others" and to assert their superiority. Thus "race" became more than a word. It became a European concept to give order to a world that seemed increasingly different, complex, and unpredictable.

Of course the "others" whom Europeans encountered were also aware that the light-skinned newcomers were different. They too began to sort out what seemed to be the various branches of humankind. If many Europeans came to think that white was good and black was evil or base, many Africans came to believe the opposite—that black was good and white was evil. Michel de Montaigne (1533–1592), a French essayist, put it well: "Each of us labels whatever is not among the customs of his own people as barbarism."

At the end of the twentieth century—at the end of the second millennium (according to the Christian calendar)—the concept of race, which has been the source of deep social, political, economic, and psychological divisions in American society, has no legitimacy among scientists. Science cannot consider traits such as intelligence, violence, or athleticism to be racial characteristics.

Discrediting old scientific theories about racial categories doesn't mean, however, that cultural differences don't exist. Skin color still matters greatly, particularly because for centuries people have behaved toward each other *as if it did*. The hand of history is upon us, and escaping the heavy weight of racial thinking is a long, painful, and often bloody process. It is one thing to observe that science has reversed itself on the matter of race. It is another to reverse human behavior once an idea is firmly lodged in the mind and is closely connected to the sorting out of political power, the division of goods, the assignment of status, and even the choice of life mates.

"The fallacy of race," warned the anthropologist Ashley Montagu a half-century ago, is "man's most dangerous myth." In the chapters ahead we will see how for the most part anonymous Americans have taken history into their own hands and have defied the official racial ideology. We will also discover how the guardians of the past have systematically written that side of our history out of the record. Throughout our history, many Rolfes and Houstons, Pocahontases and Tiana Rogers Gentrys have made their own choices and influenced their societies. This is their story.

PAUL CUFFE: AFRICAN-INDIAN SEA CAPTAIN

This is the only image we have of Paul Cuffe. It is appropriately sober for a man who had become a Quaker. An English artist drew this silhouette when Cuffe was in England just before the War of 1812. Cuffe's name is spelled with two e's. His ship *Traveller* is shown at anchor off the coast of Africa where he traded frequently. [Old Dartmouth Historical Society—New Bedford Whaling Museum.]

Kofi, an Akan-speaking African, was snatched by slavers in the 1720s on the coast of West Africa, in what today is Ghana. He was fortunate, however—if an enslaved person can be fortunate at all—to end up the property of a Massachusetts Quaker who was willing to free him when Kofi, still in his twenties, saved up his purchase price. Taking his master's name, Cuffe Slocum (in America Kofi became Cuffe) married Ruth Moses, a Wampanoag woman from Martha's Vineyard in Massachusetts, where Puritan missionaries had converted the Wampanoags to Christianity.

While raising a family of six daughters and four sons, Cuffe Slocum taught himself to read and write and became a successful farmer, ferry operator, and boatbuilder. All the while, he passed on to his children some of his deep feelings about Quakerism, his African heritage, and the Wampanoag culture of his wife. All of these influences would find expression in the life and activities of his seventh child, Paul.

Paul came to represent a rich mingling of African, Indian, and European cultures. Two years after the American Revolution, he and his brothers adopted their father's African name rather than live under the English name taken from their father's slaveowner. (Thus Paul Slocum became Paul Cuffe.) He was soon a successful merchant, trading between New England and the west coast of Africa. He promoted a back-to-Africa movement that would bring Christianity to Africa while giving African-Americans a place of refuge from white racism in early nineteenth-century America. This was his African side.

But Paul Cuffe also maintained his Native American identity. At age twenty-four he married Alice Pequit, an Indian woman. In the 1790s, Paul launched a boatbuilding and merchant business with his Indian brother-in-law, Michael Wainer, who had married Paul's sister. With Wainer, Paul sent ships out from New Bedford, Massachusetts, to the far reaches of the Atlantic world—up and down the East Coast, to France, Portugal, and to the Baltic ports of Sweden, Denmark, and Russia. Paul Cuffe also maintained close contacts with his brother Jonathan, who after marrying an Indian woman lived with her in Gay Head, a Wampanoag village on Martha's Vineyard.

Both African and Indian, Cuffe also shared in white culture. For many years he worked closely with white merchants and white abolitionists. In 1808, at age forty-nine, he joined the Westport Quaker Meeting, that congregation's only person of color. He sent one of his sons to a Quaker school in Philadelphia. Distinctly Indian and African in skin color, hair, and features, he dressed in sober Quaker gray and wore a black wide-brimmed hat. He was buried in the Quaker cemetery in Westport, Massachusetts, surrounded by headstones of white fellow Quakers. It is interesting to imagine how Africans might have viewed this tricultural man when in 1811 his ship *Traveller* arrived in Sierra Leone, on the west coast of Africa, where Cuffe recorded in his journal that "the dust of Africa lodged on our riggings."

The children of Paul and Alice Cuffe give us some idea of how the children of mixed marriages carved out their own identities—each in his or her own way. Son Paul Cuffe, Jr., followed his mother's people, referring to himself as "a Pequot Indian" in an autobiography he published many years after his father's death. But Naomi and Ruth, the two oldest daughters, married the African-American Howard brothers, recently freed from slavery, in 1806. Today the descendants of Paul Cuffe and Alice Pequit gather every five years at the Friends Meeting House in Westport, Massachusetts. Their colorations are as numerous as the voyages of this seafaring man as he traveled the world in search of bettering the human condition. "Who that justly appreciates human character," wrote the *Liverpool Mercury* after Cuffe visited the English city in 1812, "would not prefer Paul Cuffee, the offspring of an African slave, to the proudest statesman that ever dealt out destruction amongst mankind?"

THE MINGLING OF BLOOD ON
NEW WORLD FRONTIERS

"*Whether the whites won the land by treaty, by armed conquest, or, as was actually the case, by a mixture of both, mattered comparatively little so long as the land was won. It was all-important that it should be won, for the benefit of civilization and in the interests of mankind. It is, indeed, a warped, perverse, and silly morality which would forbid a course of conquest that has turned whole continents into the seats of mighty and flourishing civilized nations. All men of sane and wholesome thought must dismiss with impatient contempt the plea that these continents should be reserved for the use of scattered savage tribes, whose life was but a few degrees less meaningless, squalid, and ferocious than that of the wild beasts with whom they held joint ownership. . . . The most ultimately righteous of all wars is a war with savages . . . [that] has laid deep the foundations for the future greatness of a mighty people.*"

These words from one of America's most celebrated heroes evoke an image of the frontier that has come down to us in novels, movies, and radio and television programs. Teddy Roosevelt, the nation's twenty-sixth president, wrote them in his immensely popular *The Winning of the West*, a six-volume history that reflected the standard textbook image American

When Chief Hendrick of the Mohawk went to London in 1740, King George II presented him with elaborate apparel to help seal a diplomatic alliance. An English painter captured Hendrick in an English tricornered hat, ruffled shirt, and brocaded waistcoat. Bearing facial tattoos and holding a tomahawk, he appears as the bicultural man. He died at the Battle of Lake George in 1755, fighting alongside the British against the French. [Copyright Collection of the New-York Historical Society.]

children grew up on throughout the nineteenth century and well into the twentieth.

On the moving frontier, where red, white, and black met, the reality was far different. To be sure, the frontier was a battleground where European settlers and Indians soaked the earth with blood. But the frontier was also a meeting ground, a merging ground, and a marrying ground. Nobody left the frontier unchanged. Whether a native inhabitant of the region, a trader, trapper, soldier, settler, slave, or refugee, the people who interacted on the frontier learned from each other and leaned on each other. A South Carolina slaveholder learned rice production from his African slave. A French trader adopted the practice of wearing Indian deerskin moccasins and leggings. A runaway slave took up Choctaw hunting practices. An Abenaki woman wore French jackets. A Puritan minister learned from his African

Important English leaders, such as Colonel John Caldwell who fought with the British in the American Revolution, wore Indian apparel to signify their bond with Indian allies. Stationed at Detroit, in the heart of Indian country, Caldwell wore Indian headdress, leggings with feather moccasins, breechcloth, tomahawk, and elaborate nose and ear pendants for this portrait. [The Board of Trustees of the National Museums and Galleries on Merseyside (King's Regiment Collection).]

slave how to inoculate his children against smallpox. An Algonquian woman embraced Catholic marriage rituals. Whether red, white, or black, all the peoples who met in "the New World" had to remake themselves.

The famous historian Frederick Jackson Turner taught Americans that the frontier was "the meeting point between savagery and civilization." But today we understand that the frontier was a broad, shifting region where Indians, Europeans, and Africans—and eventually Asians—intersected. People at the time knew this. A Franciscan friar in New Mexico complained in 1631 that the Spaniards were "reared from childhood subject to the customs of [the] Indians." Fifty years later, Irish Nell, Lord Baltimore's servant in Maryland, married Charles, a full-blooded African slave, with a Catholic priest and planter families in attendance. In the 1750s, visitors to the Mohawk Valley watched Iroquois drinking tea and saw English settlers tattooing their faces. At a treaty with the Five Iroquois Nations in 1744, Pennsylvania negotiators parleyed with Tachanuntie, or Black Prince, who was half African and half Indian. "He is one of the greatest warriors that ever the Five Nations produced," reported a surprised white official, who was made to understand that Black Prince held "great sway in all the Indian councils." In 1779, a French official at Vincennes, Indiana, was amazed at how much George Rogers Clark and his straggling band of soldiers resembled Indians in their clothing.

Even if not a single drop of blood had been exchanged through racial intermixing, converging peoples from Europe, Africa, and the Americas would have traded ideas, tools, foods, animals, medicinal plants, and even on occasion children (usually as the result of raids). Thrown together, they necessarily shared with and borrowed from each other, blending their life ways and often adopting similar patterns of thought. Teddy Roosevelt could see only "scattered savage tribes" with attributes hardly different from those of "wild beasts" in the American forests. To exterminate Indians was a righteous cause that toughened the sinew of a mighty civilized people. At the end of the twentieth century, we can recognize this as what might be called "winner's history"—a reading of the past that makes the conquest of Indians seem inevitable and thereby forgives all the violence and bad faith that made it possible.

The most notable forerunners of a mestizo nation were those who lived on the trading frontiers. From the late 1500s to the late 1800s, English, Dutch, French, and Spanish fur traders in North America were the first to mix their blood with people whom many Europeans called "savages." The fur traders knew otherwise. Over several centuries, probably three-quarters of all fur traders and trappers, whatever their origins in Europe, married Indian women—in the Spanish Southwest and Florida; in French Canada, Louisiana, and the Mississippi River valley; and in English Appalachia and later in the Southwest ceded by Mexico to the Americans in 1848 after the Mexican-American War.

Most European-Indian unions were enduring and strong. Calvin Briggs, a trader in the northern Rockies, was married to Sarah Ann, a Shoshone, for thirty-three years. The marriage of Otoe Margaret Macompemay and Irish trader Andrew Drips lasted for twenty-four years. Therese, a Flathead, built her life with François Rivet on the Green River for thirty-one years. Untimely death of husband or wife broke European-Indian marriages, but little else did.

One reason these marriages worked so well was the special skills of the women. Native women's knowledge was essential to any successful trapping and trading mission. Women usually prepared the beaver pelts, deer skins, and buffalo robes that men brought into Indian villages. They also gathered wild rice, snared rabbits and quail, caught fish, drew and processed maple syrup, fashioned snowshoes, cut and sewed clothing, and served as interpreters, negotiators, and guides. Bearer of mixed-race children, the fur trader's Indian wife was indispensable as an economic and social partner. In a world of trade, she was a bridge between cultures.

A few examples illustrate the point. Thanadelthur, a Chippewa woman, served as interpreter, guide, and peace negotiator for the English as they opened the far north Hudson Bay fur trade in the early eighteenth century. A Hudson's Bay Company leader called her "the chief promoter and actor" in the extension of the fur trade that brought fortunes to English investors. A century later, Michael Laframbois, a French trader, relied on his

Jim Bridger's father-in-law, Chief Washakie, was photographed many years after his daughter had died. His plaid trade-goods shirt helped communicate his intercultural life as much as the written or spoken word. Going back more than a century, shirts of this sort made from English cloth were known as "the Indian fashion." Western Indians called Bridger "Blanket Chief" because of the red and blue robe he wore on ceremonial occasions. [National Anthropological Archives, Smithsonian Institution.]

Okanogay wife to pave the way for opening the trade with Indians in the Oregon Territory. He boasted that he was the only man "who moved with solitary security from one Umpqua village to another." The fabled Jim Bridger, who helped open Montana and Wyoming to white settlement, married three times, in each case to an Indian woman, and was widowed by each one. The daughter of Chief Washakie of the Shoshone was one of them. The equally fabled Kit Carson had four wives: an Arapaho, a Cheyenne, a Mexican, and a Taos-born Indian-Mexican woman. American textbooks shine the spotlight on intrepid western pathbreakers and Indian

The fabled western mountain man didn't have much of a chance in the 1820s and 1830s without an Indian wife. This scene, painted by the French-trained New Orleans artist Alfred Jacob Miller in 1837, shows the mountain man being accepted into the clan of his bride. [Joslyn Art Museum, Omaha, Nebraska.]

fighters, but they rarely mention that such men often married Indian wives and in the process became thoroughly Indian themselves.

Why did Indian women marry outside their own communities, taking husbands from a foreign culture? Why would they travel with trapping parties to cook for the men and mend their clothes and moccasins? In many cases, these were arranged marriages where a tribal leader would choose a daughter as a consort for a European trader. John Lawson, a Scots-Irish trader in prerevolutionary South Carolina, was sure that Indian men "are desirous (if possible) to keep their wives to themselves, as well as those in other parts of the world." But Lawson also found out that tribal chiefs provided English traders with "She-Bed-Fellows" in order to facilitate trade and cement ties between two societies. Some Indian women, however, married Europeans for their own reasons. One surviving account reports that Huron and Ottawa women in the Great Lakes region liked the French "better than their own countrymen."

In overcoming the fear and strangeness of each other's differentness, European traders and Indian women became the very symbol of mestizo America. Their unions were so numerous that new words soon entered the French and Spanish languages to describe them. *Metissage* is the French term used for the joining of Indian wives with French or English traders. Their offspring became *metis*—a term taken from the word *metisser,* "to cross." For the Spanish, the equivalent word was *mestizaje,* and the children of Spanish-Indian unions were called *mestizos.*

MILITARY FRONTIERS

Indians and Europeans also forged relationships on the military frontiers of North America. In these regions, intimate relations between allies and enemies evolved alongside the violence that frequently bloodied the frontier lands.

Born in Ireland, William Johnson immigrated to the British colonies in 1738 and settled in the Mohawk Valley, now upstate New York. He hunted, traded, and lived with the Mohawks for many years, dressing like them, participating in their war dances, smoking pipes at their councils, and taking the Mohawk name of Warraghiyagey ("Man Who Does Great Things"). "Something in his natural temper," observed a contemporary, "responds to Indian ways."

From 1755 to 1774, Johnson served as England's Superintendent of Indian Affairs. In that post, he was the key figure in gaining the support of the powerful Iroquois Confederacy in the English wars against the French.

Joseph Rolette, of French and Indian parents, represented the Pembina Metis in the Minnesota Territorial Legislature during the 1850s. He proudly displays his mixed-race identity: his hat, tie, coat, and hunting knife are French; his pants, moccasins, and tobacco pouch are Pembina. [Minnesota Historical Society.]

England's Queen Anne commissioned this full-length portrait of Sa Ga Yeath Qua Pieth Tow, one of the four Indian chiefs who made the trip to London in 1710. An intercultural diplomat, he holds an English weapon. The bear by his side symbolizes his clan; the elaborate body and facial tattoos, as well as his long, loose hunting shirt, are typically Indian. [Library of Congress.]

In the midst of the Seven Years War, Johnson met Degonwadonti. According to some accounts, she was the daughter of an important Mohawk chief and granddaughter of one of the famous Iroquois "Four Indian Kings" who traveled to London in 1710 to parley with Queen Anne about an Iroquois alliance with the English against French Canada. The English called the Mohawk chief Nichus Brant and his daughter Molly Brant. Johnson and Degonwadonti began a partnership that lasted until Johnson's death just before the American Revolution.

In joining with Johnson, Degonwadonti brought him influence, not only among the Mohawk but also with the other Iroquois nations—the Seneca, Onondaga, Oneida, and Cayuga. As a result, Johnson became what some called the only Englishman who could dominate negotiations with the five Iroquois nations. His marriage to Degonwadonti was crucial to bringing the Iroquois into the French and Indian War in 1759 on the side of the English. Johnson's importance earned him the title of baronet, given to only one other American—and he had his Mohawk wife to thank for the honor. Hearing later of the peace treaty in Paris in 1763, in which France ceded all its Canadian claims to the English, Degonwadonti could rightfully think she had helped change the map of North America.

The alliance between Degonwadonti and William Johnson lasted many years and produced eight children. Each of the mixed-race children had to work out his or her own bicultural life. At Johnson Hall, their home near the Mohawk River, west of Schenectady, Iroquois and Irish-American culture mingled. Every part of the house, Johnson said, was "constantly full of Indians." Degonwadonti and William's eldest son, Peter, received an English education in Albany, then learned French at a school in Montreal. When his father sent him to Philadelphia to learn business, he worried about losing his Mohawk language and requested a Bible that had been translated into Mohawk by his uncle. Peter's younger sisters rejected the traditional Indian dresses worn by their mother in favor of European costume and married white men. From their racially mixed parentage, each chose a separate path.

The lives of Degonwadonti and William Johnson intersected with another interracial marriage, that of her brother, Joseph Brant. In Mohawk villages Brant was known as Thayendanegea, meaning "Two Sticks of Wood Bound Together"—a fitting name for someone who lived among both the English and the Mohawks. At the age of sixteen, Joseph, who would later become a great Mohawk chief, fought in the French and Indian War. Marching with his sister's husband, William Johnson, Brant helped win a key battle over the French at Fort Niagara, for which he

The foremost Indian portraitist of the nineteenth century, George Catlin sometimes produced images of Indian chiefs he had never seen. This is the case of Thayendanegea (called Joseph Brant by the English). But he painted Brant, with scalp lock, as unmistakably Mohawk.

Gilbert Stuart, noted for portraits of George Washington and other famous white leaders, turned Brant into a version of Washington himself. With thoroughly European features, Brant seems to have changed his identity completely—at least in the artist's imagination. [New York State Historical Association, Cooperstown.]

received a British silver medal for valor. After the war, he learned English at an Indian school in Lebanon, Connecticut (the forerunner of Dartmouth College). At age thirty-one, he translated the Anglican Book of Common Prayer and the Gospel of St. Mark into Mohawk.

Like his sister, Brant helped bring two cultures closer together: He married a European, the daughter of the Irish trader George Croghan. And he sided with the British during the American Revolution. Brant understood that his people were seriously threatened by the rapidly expanding white Americans who had been swindling the Mohawks out of land for years, and he was committed to the British. Brant sailed to London in 1775 to see what the English king would offer the Iroquois for their support in the brewing war. Even from a distance of more than two hundred years, it is tempting to imagine what Brant might have said to Ethan Allen, the Vermont revolutionist who was captured after his conquest of Fort Ticonderoga and shipped to London in chains by the British aboard the same ship that Brant took. On the forty-day Atlantic passage Brant and Allen might have discussed what the war would hold for Indian-white relations.

While the stories of Molly and Joseph Brant involved interracial liaisons between allies, such unions also occurred between enemies on the military frontier. Such is the story of Eunice Williams. The daughter of John Williams, the Puritan minister of the frontier town of Deerfield, Massachusetts, Eunice was born into a world of war between the French and the English, who, since the early seventeenth century, had been competing for control of the untold riches of North America.

In 1704, when Eunice was eight, a Mohawk party allied with the French descended on Deerfield in the middle of the night, burst into the Williams home, captured the minister's family, and overpowered the entire village. The Mohawks marched the Williams family, along with a hundred other Deerfield captives, north to Montreal and then on to the Mohawk village of Kahnawahe. Eunice's mother, only six weeks from childbirth, died of exhaustion on the punishing march of more than 300 miles through snow and slush. Nineteen others died.

After two years of captivity, most of the Deerfield captives, including Eunice's father and her siblings, were sent home as part of a prisoner exchange. But Eunice chose to remain behind, living in a Mohawk village where she had been adopted by the French Catholic Indians. She soon converted to Catholicism and at sixteen married a young Mohawk. Eunice met her father's repeated attempts to convince her to return with stark refusal. She forgot English, forgot Protestantism, and forgot her biological family. In many churches of New England, and especially in her father's church, Puritans prayed for her "redemption" from "captivity." But Eunice had become Indian. She had a faithful and loving husband, gave birth to two daughters who would later marry Mohawk men, and she thought that a return to her Deerfield home would be the real captivity for her.

Years after the death of her father, Eunice reconciled with her brothers and sisters. Four times she brought her Mohawk family to visit Deerfield. Each time, however, she preferred to camp outside her brother's home, living in her own temporary dwelling, swathed in Indian blankets and beaded wampum strings, and preparing her meals separately. Known as Marguerite Arosen in Mohawk villages, she remained Mohawk. Her husband died in 1765 after half a century of marriage to his Deerfield-born wife. She died in her Mohawk village in 1785, at age eighty-nine.

Fifty-two years later, in 1837, a group of twenty-three Indians, calling themselves "Williams" (all descendants of Eunice), arrived in Deerfield to pay homage to their ancestors, the Reverend Mr. Williams and his wife. They stayed long enough to hear the current Deerfield minister deliver a moving sermon on the common origins of all human beings. Taking the text of Acts 17:26 ("The Lord hath made of one blood all nations of men for to dwell on the face of the earth") as his key, the Reverend John Fessenden sermonized that "the same life-blood circulating through the veins of every human creature, whether his skin be blanched like the snows by the chill atmosphere of the north, or darkened to a sable hue by the scorching rays of a torrid clime, purifies and reconciles all the discordant and conflicting customs and religions of Greek and Jew, Barbarian and Scythian, invites them all to one hospitable roof . . . the everlasting habitation of the same common parent, as brethren of a single, united, harmonious household."

We can only imagine what raced through the minds of the twenty-three mixed-race Williamses visiting Deerfield from their Mohawk village in Canada and through the minds of the white Deerfield churchgoers as these words came down from Reverend Fessenden's pulpit. But we do know for a certainty that the town's pastor had embraced the idea of a mestizo America. "The workings of that mysterious providence, which has mingled your blood with ours," he solemnly proclaimed to the visiting Indians, "hath made of one blood all nations of men, and hath determined the times, the places, and circumstances in which they should live, in order to accomplish his designs of impartial benevolence and general good."

SETTLEMENT FRONTIERS

While the mixing of races occurred frequently on trading and military frontiers, it happened much less on settlement frontiers, especially in England's northern colonies in North America. Coming mostly as families, Puritan and Quaker immigrants chose to live in closely knit towns. The farther inland English settlers moved, the more likely they were to cross racial boundaries. But all along the eastern seaboard, from the early 1600s to the 1800s, white settlers endeavored to re-create English society rather than mix it with others. Racial mixing occurred, but colonial leaders did not favor it, and even passed laws to forbid it between Africans and Europeans. For English settlers, patrolling racial boundaries was more important than crossing them.

By contrast, wherever the Spanish and French settled, *mestizo* or *meti* societies quickly formed. In the French Mohawk villages of Canada where Eunice Williams lived for eighty-one years, European-Indian intermixing was the rule rather than the exception. From their first arrival, the French were so few in number that they could hardly entertain a hope of survival without the friendship of the native peoples. In 1640, after four decades of colonizing, the entire French population in North America was about 270. Even a generation later, in the 1660s, the French population was only about 3,000, not more than that of several Huron towns on the upper Great Lakes, where the French were trading for furs. Friendly Indians, not enemies, were essential to French objectives. One royal governor of French Canada remarked that only two kinds of business existed in New France: the conversion of souls and the conversion of beaver into pelts. Indian partners were essential to both.

Most of the French settlers were male. Taking Indian women as mistresses, concubines, and wives, the Frenchmen felt no embarrassment at this mixing of blood and were hard put to understand English qualms about interracial relations. In Nova Scotia, where French women were very scarce, intermarriage was so common that by the late 1600s virtually all French families had Indian blood in their veins. In the more settled areas of the St. Lawrence River valley, Jesuit priests raised objections to racial mixing, but this did little to keep Frenchmen from consorting with Indian women. In spite of opposition from the Catholic Church, Louis XIV's chief minister urged the governor of New France to bring about a mingling of French and Indian cultures "in order that having but one law and one master, they may form only one people and one blood."

Far to the south, in French Louisiana, a small military garrison spawned the most ethnically and racially mixed city in North America. In the early 1700s, though they seldom married, soldiers commonly lived with enslaved Indian women. In 1717, when the French king made Louisiana a dumping ground for French criminals—mostly males—he only increased the opportunities for Frenchmen to cross racial boundaries. Within a few years, when the French king turned his royal colony over to the Company of the Indies as a private enterprise, imported African slaves soon swamped the white population. Louisiana quickly became a triracial society.

In New Orleans, for the entire eighteenth century, Africans would outnumber whites by two to one. This led to French-African liaisons and the emergence of a free black community. Alarmed by the extent of French-African intermixture, France banned intermarriage of whites and blacks in 1724, but the ban was not effective. In New Orleans, as nowhere else in North America, an urbane and talented community of *gens de couleur libres* ("free people of color") emerged—the heirs of planters and their enslaved Africans. A historian tells us their "children were sometimes educated in

France and . . . joined their white counterparts in the promotion of one of the most elegant Creole cultures in the New World."

If the French colonists of North America mingled frequently with Indians and Africans, the Spanish embraced them wholeheartedly. Like the French, the Spanish colonizers were mostly males. Without Spanish women, Spanish men could not limit their choices. In New Spain, surrounded by the Indian population, the Spanish quickly became a mixed-race people. In California, for example, only one of three male founders and one of four female founders of San Jose and San Francisco in 1777 claimed to be purely Spanish. Of Los Angeles's first forty-six residents in 1781, only two were *españoles,* or unmixed Spaniards. Much the same mixing occurred in Spanish Florida, where a visitor walking the streets of St. Augustine would have witnessed the kind of racial intermingling that had never been seen in Boston or Philadelphia.

REFUGE FRONTIERS

Mestizo America also took form in places where enslaved African-Americans fled to live among American Indians. In every part of eastern North America from the 1600s to the 1800s, escaping African slaves found refuge among Indians. White colonists, fearing an alliance of red and black peoples, strenuously promoted hatred between Indians and Africans: they offered bounties to Indians who captured escaping slaves, and tried to convince them that Africans were detestable people. Nonetheless, the bloodlines of many Indian nations were joined with those of Africa. Cherokee and Mandingo, Creek and Fula, Choctaw and Ashanti became mixed, as fugitive slaves disappeared into Indian society. The Africans took Indian spouses, produced children of mixed blood, and shared traditions.

Sometimes the offspring of such African-Indian marriages appeared in white society and even rose to places of prominence. The American Revolution was neatly bracketed by two Afro-Indians. The first blood to be shed in the Boston Massacre of 1770 was that of Crispus Attucks, whose father was African and his mother Wampanoag. Twenty years before, Attucks had escaped his slave master in Framingham, Massachusetts; later he emerged as a mariner and worker in Boston. John Adams, at the trial of the British soldiers who fired on the protesting Bostonians, called Attucks "the hero of the night." In the aftermath of the Revolution, Paul Cuffe, son of an African father and a Wampanoag mother, planned the return of black Yankees to Sierra Leone after concluding that it was nearly impossible for New England's blacks to find a life of liberty and happiness in the new republic. After marrying a Pequot woman, Cuffe became the father of black nationalism, which promoted back-to-Africa movements throughout the nineteenth and twentieth centuries.

Up and down the eastern seaboard, Indian-African intermixing continued. The whaling boat crews of Nantucket Island had many African-Indians, including the harpooners celebrated by Herman Melville in *Moby-Dick*. In Massachusetts inland towns, as well as Cape Cod and Martha's Vineyard villages, most Indians were mixed with free African-Americans by the mid-nineteenth century. On the peninsula comprising Delaware, eastern Maryland, and eastern Virginia, mixtures of Africans, Indians, and whites created deep-rooted triracial communities. Often keeping to themselves, they tried to fend off racial prejudice and remind their children of their own distinctiveness. The Wesorts of the Brandywine region of Maryland are an example. The name "Wesort" came from their efforts to differentiate "we-sort-of-people" from "you-sort-of-people." Baptismal and marriage records tell the story of seven family lines that made up the core of this mixed-race people. One family traces back to the 1670s, when an enslaved African married an Irish maidservant. Since then, black, red, and white bloodlines have been blended into the group, creating distinctive physical features. The majority of Wesorts have straight brown or black hair. Some Wesorts have Indian facial features. Blue eyes are not uncommon. From Alabama to New York, triracial societies such as the Lumbees, Red Bones, and Brass Ankles survive to this day.

The Cherokees went furthest in triracial mixing. In the early nineteenth century, the Cherokees staked their survival on adopting key white institutions such as literacy, written constitutions, family farming, and Christianity. They even adopted the practice of black chattel slavery. In the course of borrowing white ways and bringing enslaved Africans into their communities, Cherokees became much more intermixed. By the 1830s, about one-fourth of all Cherokees were intermixed, mostly with whites but many with African-Americans. Chulio, the famous Cherokee chief and warrior, was married three times: first to a Cherokee woman, then to a white woman, finally to one of his enslaved black women. In attempting to protect their homelands by being as much as possible like whites, the Cherokees passed a law in 1824 forbidding intermarriage with African-Americans. But this did not stop black-Cherokee liaisons. Today, many thousands of Americans claim both African and Cherokee descent.

RACE AND POWER

When people from different parts of the world mingle, the element of power is always at work. The white colonist almost always encountered the African as a slave after about 1660 and therefore came to think of Africans as slavelike by nature. But English settlers met the Indians on very different terms. They quickly learned how difficult it was to enslave natives in their own territory. The Indians who survived the early period of colonization usually maintained their freedom to come and go. More than that, they could be a mortal threat to the white encroacher. Though despised and feared for this, the Indian earned the grudging respect of whites. The white-Indian relationship was rarely one of master and slave, in which power was concentrated on one side. Rather, European settlers alternately traded, negotiated, formed alliances, and fought with Indians. In each case, power was divided between the two, shifting back and forth. A century after the English arrived in New England, a French observer remarked about the power of the Iroquois: "It is a strange thing that three or four thousand souls can make tremble a whole new world. New England is very fortunate in being able to stay in their good graces. New France is often desolated by their wars, and they are feared through a space of more than fifteen hundred leagues of the country of our allies."

The African, torn from his environment and transported brutally to a strange new world, had no such power to negotiate with the colonist. Unlike the native, he could hardly win the admiration of the white settler. The African rarely elicited white respect because he was caught in a brutal system of exploitation in which Europeans held most of the power.

This imbalance of power appeared also in intimate relationships. Sexual relations between European men and African women were frequent enough in the southern colonies, as anyone could tell by the growing mulatto population. But these relationships were mostly coercive, with white masters extracting sexual favors from enslaved females by force or intimidation. As the white female population grew, such sexual liaisons became socially repugnant in white society. Farther north, where slaves were fewer in number and white women more available, white men practiced interracial sex less and were more likely to condemn it. By the time of the American Revolution, all the colonies had banned black-white marriage. These laws not only indicated official distaste for racial intermingling but raised a barrier against what white men feared most: English women consorting voluntarily with African men.

Bans on interracial marriage did not, however, stop the sexual aggressions and passions of white male slave owners. Nor were they intended to. To ban racial intermarriage was simply a way of stating with legal finality that the African, even when free, was not the equal of the white man. Racial intermingling outside of marriage, so long as it involved white men and black women, was not an expression of equality but rather an often brutal proclamation of the superior rights of white men.

The unrestrained sexual contact that European men had with African women, especially in the South, had no parallel in the case of Indian women. If an Indian woman chose to share her bed with a white man, it was usually on mutually agreeable terms. Most often, it involved emotional commitment and marriage, just as in the case of Pocahontas and John Rolfe, or Mary Musgrove and her white husbands (see profile, page 44). White women seldom married Indian men because native men were rarely present in settler communities. Similarly, Indian men rarely prized European women. It is telling that the English colonists, with rare exceptions, saw no reason to ban interracial marriage between Europeans and

Indians at the same time they were prohibiting black-white intermarriage.

Thomas Jefferson, drafter of the Declaration of Independence, made clear the difference in white attitudes toward Africans and Indians. When serving his first term as president, Jefferson promoted his belief that "the ultimate point of rest and happiness" for Native Americans was "to let our settlements and theirs meet and blend together, to intermix and become one people. . . . This," Jefferson explained, "is what the natural progress of things will . . . bring on, and it will be better to promote than to retard it." However, Jefferson entertained no such belief in the "natural progress of things" when it came to black-white intermingling. Five years after drafting the Declaration of Independence, he wrote that it was unthinkable to incorporate freed Africans into white society. When freed, Africans must be "removed beyond the reach of mixture." Five years from death, in 1821, he clung to this view that "nothing is more certainly written in the book of fate than that the two races, equally free, cannot live in the same government." Yet if the nation's third president could never overcome his belief in the innate inferiority of people of African descent, other Americans, even in his own lifetime, would imagine how the nation's polyglot residents would become "one people."

MARY MUSGROVE:
POWER BROKER OF THE EARLY SOUTH

In the Creek villages of South Carolina and Georgia, she was Princess Coosaponakeesa. In Charleston and Savannah, she was Mary Musgrove, then Mary Matthews, finally Mary Bosomworth. A child of the fur trade whose Scots-Irish father had married a Creek woman, she was the most important bridge between whites and Indians on the southeastern frontier from the 1720s to the 1750s, and one of the largest landowners in the prerevolutionary South. Coosaponakeesa grew up both Indian and white; she maintained both her Indian and English identity, but she lived mostly in the white world after her first marriage.

Born about 1700 in Coweta, the main war town of the Lower Creeks, Coosaponakeesa inherited great status in the Creek Nation because her mother was the sister of Brims, the principal Creek chief. In Creek society, one derived status not from one's father's position but from one's mother's lineage. Her white father took her to an English Carolina settlement when she was seven, and there she learned English, was baptized in an Anglican church, and practiced English ways.

In her early twenties, Coosaponakeesa married Johnny Musgrove, also a fur-trade child whose father, a wealthy South Carolina planter, had married a Creek woman. For seven years Mary and Johnny Musgrove lived in a Creek-Yamacraw village where they established a trading post and became the chief negotiators of peaceful relations between the expanding South Carolina settlements and the nearby Indians. After 1732, when James Oglethorpe arrived from England to establish the colony of Georgia, Mary Musgrove became his treasured interpreter and negotiator. Through her, Oglethorpe secured treaties and land concessions from the Creeks and Yamacraws.

After Johnny Musgrove's death, in 1735, Mary married her former

No likeness of Mary Musgrove has ever been discovered, but she had close relations with Tomochici, king of the Yamacraws (shown here). Mary Musgrove lived in the Yamacraw settlement, near the present site of Savannah, after marrying Johnny Musgrove, her first husband, in about 1725. This portrait was done in 1734. Tomochici's nephew, son of the neighboring Etchita chief, holds a bald eagle, later to become an American symbol. [National Anthropological Archives, Smithsonian Institution.]

indentured servant, Jacob Matthews, who commanded twenty rangers at her trading house sixty miles upriver from Savannah. There, Mary kept an eye on the hostile Spanish to the south while maintaining Creek loyalty to the English. Seven years later, after her second husband died, Mary married the Anglican minister of Savannah, Thomas Bosomworth. A skilled negotiator, and by now one of the largest landowners in Georgia, Mary Bosomworth continued her role as the chief diplomat maintaining Creek-English relations on a stable footing.

White colonists were learning to sneer at what they called "half-breeds." But in many places and through many decades they relied on such mixed-race people as Mary Musgrove to link Indian and English societies together. In reality, Mary Musgrove was a "double-breed," extraordinarily important for two societies precisely because she was fully English and fully Creek.

RACE IN THE AMERICAS:
THE SPANISH AND ENGLISH DIFFERENCE

In 1526, five years after Hernán Cortés defeated Moctezuma, emperor of the Aztec empire, the Spanish conquistador arranged the marriage of Moctezuma's daughter to an important Spanish official. The seventeen-year-old Aztec princess Tecuichpotzin, named Isabel by the Spanish, became the model of a Hispanicized Indian. Her children came to represent the mixing of races in New Spain and the creation of a new society. In the following years, Isabel had three Spanish husbands and bore seven mestizo children. Becoming a devout Catholic, the Aztec princess bridged the worlds of Spaniard and Aztec. She became the symbol of *mestizaje,* the Spanish term for the mingling of races. Her daughter married the discoverer of the fabulous silver mines of Zacatecas, and her granddaughter married Juan de Oñate, the colonizer and governor of New Mexico, on New Spain's northern frontier. Most of Isabel's sons married Spanish women and became part of the colonial nobility in Mexico. With Spanish-Aztec blood mingled from the beginning in their society, many Mexicans came to celebrate *mestizaje* and turned Isabel into a symbolic national figure.

TWO RACIAL ENCOUNTERS

Anyone who has traveled to Mexico, Venezuela, Nicaragua, Cuba, or Brazil quickly sees that the mixing of races in Latin America has been far more common than in the United States and Canada. Along with Hawaii, Latin America is the area of the world where the most extensive intermingling of peoples in human history has taken place. The census figures of modern South America confirm this. They show that only 20 percent of Venezuelans are classified as white, that only one of nine Panamanians is racially unmixed, and that a large majority of Mexicans combine Indian, Spanish, and African elements.

Why is this so? For many years, historians have advanced two explanations. First, even before Columbus reached the Americas, the Spanish and Portuguese had interacted with people of different cultures, particularly with dark-skinned people, whereas the English did not. Centuries of war and trade with Berbers, Moors, and other people of the Middle East and North Africa shaped Spanish and Portuguese culture. Some Spanish and Portuguese people already had mixed ancestries. The English, by contrast, had remained within their island fortress. Sheltered from other cultures, they were predisposed toward viewing interracial contacts with suspicion and even alarm.

A second explanation is that when Spanish and Portuguese colonists reached the New World, they lived under church and government rules that made racial intermixing easier. The Catholic Church had permissive attitudes toward non-Christian people; their system of law protected the rights of slaves and insisted on their dignity; and the Spanish and Portuguese monarchies adopted policies that encouraged at least some respect for Indian and African peoples. By contrast, English Protestantism was unusually rigid against admittance of non-Christian, "savage" people to the church. English law had nothing to say on the subject of enslavement, leaving colonists free to create the most unbending laws to contain their bound laborers and strip them of dignity. And English government exercised much less authority in its colonies, especially in the matter of treating enslaved non-English groups.

In recent years, historians have added a third explanation for differing patterns of racial intermixing in the Americas. In this view, it was the conditions in the New World, not patterns in the Old, that exerted the most influence.

In America, from the very beginning most Spanish males arrived without Spanish women. Therefore, they began to mix with Indian women. The Spanish labor system greatly aided this. *Encomenderos,* men who had distinguished themselves in the eyes of the Spanish king by contributing to the conquest of the Indians, were supposed to provide for and protect the Indians. But in reality, they often pressed Indians into household service where native people were in constant contact with Spanish settlers, living side by side with them in their *haciendas.* Since Spanish women were scarce among the conquistadores, Spanish men looked to Indian women for romance and sexual pleasure. Either through concubinage or marriage, Indian women became central to Spanish colonial life. Just nine years after Columbus's first voyage across the Atlantic, the Spanish king put the royal seal of approval on Spanish-Indian intermarriage.

Spanish colonial society recognized the children born of these Indian-Spanish matings without embarrassment. They were simply mixed-race children, called *mestizos* from the beginning. Spaniards widely agreed that mestizo children were inferior to pure-blooded Spanish offspring, yet they could occupy an important place in colonial society. As early as 1650, as mestizos began to outnumber pure-blooded Spaniards in New Spain, the idea of mixed-race people was becoming the norm. More than almost anything else, *mestizaje* would distinguish New Spain from Old Spain.

Yet as common as *mestizaje* was, Spanish racial crossing did not end privilege built on racial bias. Punishments were handed out more severely to Indians, Africans, or mixed-race people than to pure-blood Spaniards. *Españoles* lived in Spanish-American towns near the plaza, while mixed-race people, along with Indians and Africans, clustered on the edge of town or in designated neighborhoods. In some parts of Spanish America, militia companies kept *españoles* separate from mestizos and mulattoes. Social status was not fixed solely by race, but race counted. Still, for the Spanish, the maintenance of racial boundaries was less important than it was for the English.

The history of Spanish-African mixing is similar, yet different. The Spanish (and the Portuguese) brought enslaved Africans to their New World colonies much earlier than did the English in North America. What is more, they brought Africans in larger numbers proportionate to European settlers. The Spanish used Africans as craftsmen, supervisors of enslaved Indians, and even as militiamen. This gave African males a degree of respect, a status much above that of field laborer. This respect, limited though it was, extended to African women, making them acceptable partners. Status-seeking Spaniards doubtlessly shunned marriage with Africans, and some colonial officials even tried to obtain a royal ban on African-Spanish intermarriage. But all such attempts were doomed. Nobody, as one historian puts it, "was successful in keeping Spaniards, Indians, and Africans out of each other's gene pools."

Throwing together large numbers of Africans and Indians with smaller numbers of mostly male Spaniards created continuous racial blending as well as a mingled civilization. With no prohibitions against interracial contact and interracial marriage, the Spaniards, Africans, and Indians intermixed extensively. This did not end racial prejudice. The offspring of mixed-race marriages could expect a life of discrimination and thwarted ambition. And those with African ancestry faced more limited chances than those with Indian bloodlines. Above all, Spanish blood counted the most. Not for many generations would Mexicans begin to celebrate "the cosmic race" that came through the fusion of African, Indian, and Spanish blood. But if prejudice remained, the fusion continued, often unruly and always unpredictable.

PICTURING SPANISH AMERICA

A series of family portraits produced in eighteenth-century Mexico provides a fascinating record of colonial Spanish attitudes toward *mestizaje*. In a day when European portrait painters worked almost exclusively for wealthy patrons, these depictions of everyday life and ordinary families are very unusual. Known as "casta paintings," these images of racially inter-

The *castas mexicanos*, or Mexican caste paintings, date back to the 1720s. People seem to have stopped painting them after Mexican independence from Spain in 1810. [Sir Edward Hulse, Breamore House, Hampshire, England.]

mixed families show that by the 1700s the Mexicans were eager to advertise the remarkable blending of racial types in the New World—virtually the signature of Spain's conquest of the exotic southern half of the Americas.

The painting above, for example, captures a quiet scene between a very light-skinned Spanish man and a brown-skinned Indian woman. Their children, the caption tells us, are "Mestizo," half Spanish and half Indian. While the artist's words tell us nothing else about this family, the painting itself speaks volumes. The Indian woman is clad in the attire of an upper-class or noble Spanish woman. Her dress is of fine printed fabric and adorned with lace at the sleeves and collar. She wears a white lacy head covering and is graced by a pearl choker and a many-stranded bracelet. The painting invites the viewer to conclude that this full-blooded Indian woman has acquired high status and wealth, befitting her husband's social position as indicated by his wig and elegant clothes. Pocahontas in London wore such splendid attire, and William Johnson's Mohawk wife did also; but rare were the Indian women in the English colonies who could have attained such status. Sent back to Spain as souvenirs, such paintings legitimized interracial marriage.

Casta paintings of Spanish men and African women portray a less optimistic story. The artist of the picture on the facing page introduces view-

FORBIDDEN LOVE

ers to a Spanish man, his African wife, and their mulatto son in a dark kitchen of a small apartment. While the mother works, her son seems preoccupied with his plate of food and the father seems to be rolling a cigarillo for himself. None of the family are elaborately dressed. The wife wears a simple kerchief and plain skirt. This reflected the lower social position that most mulattoes would occupy.

We see a dignified marriage between a Spanish man and his mulatto wife

Mexican painters of interracial families chose domestic settings for their portraits, which were often fanciful. In this case, the artist was much more realistic. [Museo de America, Madrid.]

Relatively few mixed-race people from Nueva España crossed the Atlantic to visit Spain, so Spaniards formed their impressions of the new population in their colonies from paintings such as these. [Sir Edward Hulse, Breamore House, Hampshire, England.]

in the painting above. Their *morisca* (three-quarters Spanish, one-quarter African) daughter is fair-skinned. Like her mother, she wears a pearl choker and earrings. In actuality, most mixed marriages in New Spain were between people of the artisan or laboring class, who would not have appeared in public attired quite so stylishly as this painting suggests.

Though not shy about crossing racial boundaries, Spanish colonists paid close attention to blood. In the painting on the facing page, the artist depicts a wealthy-looking Spaniard with an equally wealthy *morisca* woman. The suckling child, only one-eighth African, is blond with very light skin, and therefore called *albino,* meaning "white." This painting illustrates the Spanish notion that a predominance of Spanish blood, trans-mitted through the mother's milk, is capable of wiping away the small portion of "contaminated" African blood. The man's velvet coat and frilled shirt cuffs are matched by his wife's elegant gown, trimmed with ribbons and lace. She wears pearl earrings and a necklace.

The unions of Spaniards and *albinos* sometimes led to children who, though only one-sixteenth African, often had darker skin than either parent. Such a child was labeled *torna atrás*, meaning "turn back" or "throw back"—that is, a throwback to the color of an African grandparent or great-grandparent. The artist of the picture at the top of page 54 invites the viewer to conclude that this was not an embarrassment. In a contented family setting where the child is darker than either parent, her father rolls cigarettes. "Turning back" happened in a variety of genetic combinations. The title of the painting at the bottom of page 54 tells that a *lobo* husband

The Spanish thought that three generations of crossing with a Spaniard would cleanse the blood of Indians and Africans. The child of this union would be considered white. The English gradually moved in the direction of categorizing anyone with a single drop of African blood, such as this child, as black. [Sir Edward Hulse, Breamore House, Hampshire, England.]

Seeking wives, most Spanish men preferred a woman such as the one portrayed here, who was part Spanish rather than purely Indian or African. Blood always counted for Spanish colonists but differently than in the English colonies. [Museo Nacional de Ethnologia, Madrid.]

Spanish colonists invented many terms to describe different degrees of racial mixing. In this painting, the Indian wife of a *lobo* husband bears a *lobo* child, but other terms for such an offspring were also used. [Sir Edward Hulse, Breamore House, Hampshire, England.]

(from an Indian mother and African or mixed-race father) and his Indian wife produce a *lobo,* "which is a return backwards."

Since the mixing of Spanish men with Indian and African women was mainly prompted by the absence of Spanish women, it is surprising to find portraits of Spanish women with African or Indian men. Still, as seen in the picture below, a simply dressed Spanish woman is married to a man of pure African blood, decked out in a brocaded jacket. In another painting, a wealthy Spanish woman, portrayed in an ermine cape and dazzling jewelry, looks lovingly at her four mulatto children, two daughters and two sons. The art on page 56 pictures a Spanish woman and her *castizo* husband looking fondly at their son, who is labeled "Spanish," reflecting the Spanish view that three blood steps from an Indian parent "purifies" the offspring, making the child fully Spanish.

Most Spanish women had many suitors in a society where they were greatly outnumbered by Spanish men. Since they were prized, very few Spanish females married African men. However, the *casta* painters were not shy about representing such marriages. [Museo Nacional, Mexico.]

In Mexico, the children of racially mixed marriages, or even pure-blooded Indians, sometimes achieved great success. One example was Benito Juarez, a full-blooded Indian who became president of the nation in 1861. No parallel for this occurred in the United States. [Museo de America, Madrid.]

De Meſtizoy India; Coyote

This casta painter faithfully portrayed the low social status of most mixed-race Mexicans. In a class-conscious culture, Spaniards regulated fabrics and even colors so that the wearer's clothes made evident his or her social place. [Elizabeth Waldo-Denzel, Multi-Cultural Music and Art Foundation, Northridge, CA.]

In depicting everyday life, the artists portrayed many mixed-race families in humble settings, which was certainly the reality of eighteenth-century Mexican life. Most of the casta paintings showing families in working-class garb involved husbands and wives with various degrees of African and Indian blood. Finery, grand homes, and genteel manners appear to have been reserved for families where one partner was purely Spanish. The other partner—of African, Indian, or mixed blood—could aspire to wealth and status through marriage but could not be the source of upper-class status. In the painting above, a pure-blood Indian woman, married to a mestizo man, carries a swaddled *coyote* child while another child rides a donkey. The tattered clothes of both parents signify lower-class status.

Most artists produced their casta paintings in series of sixteen variations of interbreeding, as on page 59, though some painters constructed tableaus of eight or twelve. European collectors could quickly see that a Spanish and Indian couple had a *mestizo* child; that *mestizo* and Spanish mates produced *castizo* children; that the offspring of Spanish and mulatto parents was a *morisco;* that the child of a *morisco* and Spanish marriage was a *chino,* or *albino;* that a *chino* and Indian pair sired a child that was termed *salta atrás,* literally "to jump back"—or away—from Spanish blood. And so forth, even to the point of racial entanglements so perplexing that the resulting child was *tente en el aire* ("hold yourself in the air") or *no te entiendo* ("I don't understand you"), a mixing of blood impossible to unscramble.

On the positive side, these casta paintings, mostly portraying interracial families in serene domestic and workaday settings, invited tolerance, compassion, and some understanding of the fundamental unity of the human race. The widespread distribution of these casta paintings, often taken back or sent to Spain as mementos of the exotic new world, spread the view that interracial mixing was not offensive but was rather the natural path of human affairs when three worlds met.

Yet the casta paintings also tell the story that the Spanish colonists paid careful attention to racial distinctions and certainly believed in their own racial superiority. As one German observer in Mexico put it, "Any white person, although he rides barefoot, imagines himself to be of the nobility of the country." The paintings also hint at the belief that Spanish blood was essential to the civilized person and African blood leads toward degeneracy. As a Spaniard in Mexico explained, "If the mixed-blood is the offspring of a Spaniard and an Indian, the stigma disappears at the third step in descent . . . [whereas] a mulatto can never leave his condition of mixed blood but rather it is the Spanish element that is lost and absorbed into the condition of a Negro. . . ." Thus the casta paintings, in a society where policing racial boundaries was impossible, tried to impose some order by classifying mixtures of races.

A few of the casta paintings show couples fighting, something virtually unknown in other paintings at this time. The portrait painters, reflecting the Spanish racial mentality, especially associated such clashes with the mixing of African and Indian bloodstreams. While the dark-skinned African or Indian who married a light-skinned Spaniard could expect a child with a favorable temperament, the children of African and Indian parents could

One can imagine how this sixteen-part painting of racial mixing in Nueva España would have occasioned interest if hung on the wall of a merchant in Seville in about 1750. Today, many such paintings are in private collections in Spain, Mexico, France, and the United States. [Museo del Virreinato, Mexico.]

usually be counted on to be saucy, wild, lazy—or even a criminal. In one casta series, for example, a painting is inscribed, "In the Americas people of different colours, customs, temperaments, and languages are born: born of the Spaniard and the Indian woman is a mestizo, who is generally humble, tranquil, and straightforward." A second painting announces, "The pride and sharp wits of the mulatto are instilled by his white father and black mother." But in another family portrait, "the Jibaro born of Indian mother and Calpamulato father is restless and almost always arrogant." While yet another warns that "from lobo and Indian woman, the cambujo is usually slow, lazy, and cumbersome." Still more dire is this prediction: "From black father and Indian mother, the lobo is bad blood: thieves and pick-pockets."

Even some of the names used for children of mixed Indian and African parentage were ominous. *Lobo* (wolf) was the term used for the child of an African-Indian marriage. In the painting below, a mulatto woman seizes

Notice how the wife's and husband's clothes and the simple setting signal the lower-class status of a marriage in trouble. *Casta* painters never associated such domestic quarreling with upper-class families, though domestic disputes and family violence were not confined to those at the bottom of society. [Museo Nacional, Mexico.]

the hair of her *coyote* husband (born of an Indian-mestizo marriage, thus three-quarters Indian) and threatens to crown him with a wooden bowl. In another painting of an Indian male with mestizo wife and *coyote* child, pictured barefooted in a humble setting, the inscription warns against certain kinds of racial intermingling. The child of the mulatto-*coyote* union is labeled *ahí te estas*—"stay where you are"—a warning about certain forms of mixture, particularly when no Spanish blood was involved.

PICTURING ENGLISH AMERICA

In Britain's American colonies, there was nothing like the casta paintings. Indeed, artists and publishers of such paintings would probably have been expelled from colonial towns, nor could they have expected to find a market for the sixteen-part racial mixing series produced by many artists in cities such as Mexico City. When we understand the reasons for this, we will have unlocked the key to the peculiar form of racial thinking that developed in North America.

As we have seen in chapter 2, racial intermingling did occur, especially in frontier zones and particularly in the southern colonies, where by the mid 1700s Africans represented half of the population. Yet most English colonists hated the idea of living in a place where interracial relationships might become the norm. Whereas the Spanish could accept this and even advertise it as a mark of a new society forming in the Americas, the English found it intolerable. A very different context planted the seeds of the watertight racial compartments—white, red, or black—where in-betweenness was not an option. English painters could certainly have found white women married to black men, white men married to Indian women, and the mixed-race children of interracial marriages married to other mixed-race persons or persons of purely African, Indian, English, German, or Dutch heritage. But painting such family portraits would have promoted exactly what the leaders of colonial society were determined to avoid and refused to acknowledge.

The portraits by colonial painters illustrate the resistance to the idea of

John Copley (standing) paid close attention to clothing as a marker of refinement in this family portrait. Copley portrays himself and his family as models of politeness and cultured behavior. [John Singleton Copley, *The Copley Family*, Andrew W. Mellon Fund, copyright 1998 Board of Trustees, National Gallery of Art, Washington, D.C., 1776/1777.]

fluid racial boundaries across which people could easily and legitimately cross. Artists did family portraits on contract—almost always for wealthy families and never for popular consumption. The painting above is typical of prerevolutionary Boston. A painter himself, John Copley executed portraits of numerous wealthy colonists, but he would have found it inconceivable to graphically present racial mixing. English painters captured the images of a few Indians and Africans but only as single figures, such as Lapowinsa, a Delaware Indian chief (facing page, top), or Absalom Jones, a black minister who founded the first African Episcopal church after the American Revolution (facing page, bottom). In the artistic record as in social life, English painters kept the races separate.

No English term for *mestizaje* ever appeared in spite of the racial mixing that occurred before the eyes of Anglo-American settlers. The dominant group instead defined all mixed-race people as either Africans or Indians. There could be no intermediate social compartments—*mulatto, mestizo,*

Lapowinsa was one of the few Indians painted in Pennsylvania. Gustavus Hesselius, a German immigrant, shows Lapowinsa with a chipmunk hide pouch, often used to carry a tobacco pipe or other European trade item. Hesselius did this sensitive portrait in 1732. [The Historical Society of Pennsylvania.]

Absalom Jones purchased his freedom by working late into the night for many years in his master's store in Philadelphia. His dignified pose and somber apparel befit his rise from self-taught slave to eminent leader of the nation's largest free African-American community in the early nineteenth century. [Delaware Art Museum, Gift of the Absalom Jones School, 1965.]

castizo, and so forth. Only extreme categories would do—black, white, Indian. The child of an English-Cherokee marriage would always be Indian. The child of an African-English marriage would always be black. A white woman could give birth to a black or Indian infant, who would be classified as black or Indian, but a black or Indian woman could never produce a white child. In Spanish colonies spaces were provided for a variety of mixed-race people; in-betweenness was perfectly legitimate and even advertised. To the English mind, no room existed for sanctioned racial mixing or for a range of racial categories. For generations to come, this peculiar construction of race and racial attitudes would plague Euro-Americans, enslaved Africans, free blacks, and American Indians.

The United States of the Disunited Races

In April 1831, subscribers to William Lloyd Garrison's fiery abolitionist journal *The Liberator* read a chilling account—by "T.T."—of two dreams. In his first dream, the anonymous writer described how Americans of all colors were living in harmony and had come to regard skin color as insignificant. "We are completely united into one people," he explained, "and there is as little thought of separate interests and feelings between blacks and whites, as between tall and short, or dark eyes and blue, or between men and women." T.T. found himself present at an elegant reception where the newly elected president of the United States was to be introduced. "Nearly one half the company were of the negro race," he related, and "blacks and whites were mingling with perfect ease in social intercourse." When the president-elect arrived, T.T. discovered he was a distinguished African-American.

Upon asking how the nation had overcome its racial prejudices, T.T. was told that the creation of equal economic opportunity for black Americans had dissolved color and class barriers. This paved the way for interracial marriage. "Cash balanced color in the accounts of society and proved a passport to gentility," explained one guest. Another guest, an old man, remembered how in his youth it was said that it was impossible that blacks "should ever mingle upon equal terms with the whites. It was considered fixed as the decrees of fate, that they must always continue a distinct and degraded race." The reception ended with a discussion about "whether the national character had not been improved . . . by the union of the two races." All agreed that "Whites had gained a certain ease and dignity . . . in manners" and that "intercourse with the milder [African] race" softened white "pugnacious" instincts for competition. African-Americans, on the other hand, had developed "a more active and enterprising spirit." Blending together, the two races had created a multiracial culture that benefited all and brought social peace to the nation.

In the second dream, T.T. found his town's citizens terror-stricken as enslaved black insurrectionists launched an all-out war to end slavery. Securing the support of the Cherokees and the black Haitian government, which had overthrown French slavery three decades before, they were attacking everywhere. Free northern blacks rushed south to help break the chains of their brethren. Desperately trying to overpower the rebellious blacks, white soldiers hanged fifty captured insurrectionists. Escaped slaves retaliated, hanging fifty white prisoners. Soon the black rebels moved north. Descending upon T.T.'s town, they stormed his house and butchered his wife and child "before my face." Soon the United States government capitulated. T.T., like all other whites, found himself enslaved by the victorious and vengeful African-Americans. "We were fastened two and two together, and worked incessantly in the broiling sun, the least pause of weariness being followed by the lash."

His world turned upside down, T.T. found himself in Charleston, South Carolina, where an "imperial council" of former slaves debated what to do with the now-enslaved population of former white oppressors. The black leaders discussed alternatives for dealing with their white captives: perpetual enslavement, colonization in Turkey, or the execution of all former slaveholders. The victorious blacks rejected the offer of a treaty with the surviving whites that would have guaranteed white prisoners life and liberty, because "our allies, the Cherokees," said the blacks, "would laugh to scorn the idea of trusting to a treaty."

The dreams of the anonymous T.T., published just four months before Nat Turner unleashed a bloody slave insurrection in Virginia, reflected two streams within the new American nation in the first half of the nineteenth century. One current urged the nation toward a mestizo America in which racial intermingling would blur distinctions between the races and make the notion of *mestizaje* entirely acceptable. The other current, much stronger as it turned out, led toward harshly negative racial attitudes on the part of whites, propelling a vision of an American branch of the Anglo-Saxon race that would spread across the continent, determined to prevent the mixing of people of different racial ancestries.

The contrast between T.T.'s two dreams illustrated the nation's basic split. Between the American Revolution and the Civil War, these two competing visions of America—one of racial separation, the other of racial mingling—clashed. To this day, the tension between these two views continues to shape American lives, beliefs, and policies. In treating the period between American independence and the outbreak of a tragic war between North and South, our history books dwell on expansion to the West, the rise of King Cotton and slavery in the South, northern industrialization, the age of democratic politics, and antebellum reform movements inspired by the Second Great Awakening. But our textbooks tell us little about how the question of race mixing was stitched into all these broad developments. We will see that as the first two generations of post-independence Americans sorted out their racial future, they moved in a perilous direction. Hardening positions on race and the burning question of slavery became thoroughly entangled.

RACE AND THE REVOLUTIONARY GENERATION

"Can America be happy?" asked Tom Paine, the Revolution's most widely read pamphleteer. "As happy as she please," he replied. "She hath a blank sheet to write upon." In this simple prose, Paine reminded the Americans that they stood at a fateful moment—when they might begin anew, reinvent America, create whatever kind of society they wanted, construct a government entirely of their own devising. "We have it in our power to begin the world over again," Paine counseled the revolutionists. "A situation similar to the present has not happened since the days of Noah until now. The birthday of a new world is at hand."

In conducting the war against England, the Americans confronted awesome decisions. How would each state construct a constitution to live under? What powers should be given to a central government? Should women and landless men have a vote? What policy should govern relations with the powerful Indian nations on the new republic's borders? How would the western lands, whether purchased or obtained by force, be distributed and governed? Should slavery be abolished? How would people of different ancestries and different social conditions live together? How would a polyglot people answer the question of the French visitor Hector Saint John de Crèvecoeur: "What then is the American, this new man"? Would they fulfill Crèvecoeur's prediction that "here individuals of all nations are melted into a new race of men, whose labours and posterity will one day cause great changes in the world"?

An answer to some of these questions was encoded in preambles to state constitutions and in preambles to laws passed by state legislatures. Pennsylvania's 1780 Gradual Abolition Act began with a ringing statement: "It is not for us to enquire why, in the creation of mankind, the inhabitants of the several parts of the earth were distinguished by a difference in feature or complexion—it is sufficient to know that all are the work of an Almighty hand." This statement certainly echoed Paine's optimism about re-creating America in the revolutionary era. While winning independence from their English masters, some whites came to believe that all people were born equal, equal not only in rights acquired at birth but with the same potential and the same basic moral and intellectual capacity. Only man-made institutions, or ideas, made people different. Slavery was one. Slavery degraded Africans and forced them into labor where their true talents could not emerge. They had equal endowments by nature but were crippled by backbreaking work and horrific brutality.

Many revolutionists were certain that a new, freedom-loving republic could never be based on slavery. In making their argument for abolishing slavery, they worked hard to prove that Africans were not inferior by birth and, if freed, would become able and worthy citizens. Philadelphia's famous doctor Benjamin Rush publicized the talents of the black physician James Derham, who was born into slavery in Philadelphia and sold to a Quaker doctor who taught him medicine. After passing through the hands of at least four other slave masters, Derham was freed in New Orleans and began practicing as a doctor. When he came to Philadelphia in the late 1780s, Rush spread the word of Derham's vast medical knowledge.

Another antidote to the common belief that enslaved Africans were forever inferior was the widely publicized story of Thomas Fuller, called the "African Calculator." Though brought to North America as a fourteen-year-old slave and consigned to lifelong labor in Virginia, the African-born Fuller could perform spectacular arithmetic calculations. Hearing of his genius, doubting whites contrived impossible problems for an illiterate slave: How many seconds has a man lived after 70 years, 17 days, and 12 hours? Reflecting for a moment, Fuller spat back: 2,210,500,800 seconds. (When his white interrogators charged him with a small error, he stunned them by pointing out that they had forgotten to account for leap years.) How many sows would a farmer have if he started with six and each sow had six female pigs in the first year and they all increased in the same proportion to the end of eight years? Fuller pondered briefly. Back came the answer: 34,588,806. When he died in 1790 at age eighty, antislavery newspaper editors proclaimed that if only ordinary opportunities had come his way, instead of a lifetime in slavery, "neither the Royal Society of London, the Academy of Sciences at Paris, nor even a Newton himself, need have been ashamed to acknowledge him as a brother in science."

A year after the death of the "African Calculator," Benjamin Banneker, the self-taught black astronomer in Maryland, published an almanac that gave the lie to white arguments about supposedly inferior Africans. Full of elegant astronomical calculations about the movement of heavenly bodies, Banneker's book astounded whites. How could Banneker have taught himself the spherical trigonometry required for these calculations? Benjamin Franklin's grandson, editor of a Philadelphia newspaper, published an essay on the remarkable Banneker, making the point that he was "fresh proof

Benjamin Banneker's father had been brought to Maryland from Guinea as a slave and later received his freedom. His mother was the daughter of an English indentured servant who had married a freed slave in Maryland. Banneker was born free. His English grandmother used the Bible to teach him to read and write.

that the powers of the mind are disconnected with the colour of the skin, or, in other words, a striking contradiction to . . . [the] doctrine that the Negroes are naturally inferior to the whites, and unsusceptible of attainments in arts and sciences." In 1795, after surveying his friends, a prominent Massachusetts minister, Jeremy Belknap, agreed: "It is neither birth nor colour, but education and habit, which forms the human character."

By the time the Constitutional Convention met in 1787, white reformers were insisting, as the Book of Genesis held, that humanity was composed of a single species and that all human variation arose from climate, upbringing, or external circumstances. But others argued the opposite. Jefferson repeated stereotypical white ideas of inborn black inferiority in his *Notes on the State of Virginia*. Nature, he wrote, had made Africans much inferior to whites or Indians in both body and mind. Hoping to change Jefferson's mind, Banneker sent a copy of his almanac to the sage of Monticello, urging him to help African-Americans "who have long laboured under the abuse and censure of the world . . . and have long been considered rather as brutish than human, and scarcely capable of mental endowments."

As the new nation searched for its unique identity, the belief in one universal race gradually began to fade. The belief that mankind was divided into superior and inferior races grew stronger, and racial mixing became a subject of national concern. During the Federal Constitutional Convention (held in Philadelphia), Pennsylvania's James Wilson admitted his "apprehensions . . . from the tendency of the blending of the blacks with the whites." South Carolina's William Loughton Smith went further, declaring that any "mixture of the races would degenerate the whites." If African-Americans intermarried "with the whites, then the white race would be extinct, and the American people would be all of the mulatto breed." From this concern with maintaining the purity of white blood in the new republic, various northern states nervously considered laws banning interracial marriage. New York's assembly passed such a law in 1785, but the upper house objected because "the free subjects of this State ought to be left to their free choice." In 1786, Massachusetts ruled illegal all marriages between whites and blacks or whites and Indians. Rhode Island followed suit in 1798. In the South, laws prohibiting interracial marriage were already on the books. Jefferson, in Virginia, wanted to go further, banishing from the state white women who bore mulatto children.

It says volumes about Thomas Jefferson's tortured thoughts on race that he made no proposal that his state should banish the mothers of mulatto children if the mother was black rather than white. Jefferson had been involved since the late 1780s in a sexual liaison with his slave Sally Hemings. Sally herself was the half-sister of Jefferson's deceased wife, since they had a grandfather in common. Sally certainly bore one and almost certainly bore at least five of Jefferson's children, none of whom he admitted were his. Condemning racial intermingling while engaging in it himself (as did many members of his family), his "rational" side condemned what his emotional side embraced. With a few exceptions, Jefferson's biographers have long denied his relationship with Sally Hemings, spouting that such a liaison was "virtually unthinkable in a man of Jefferson's moral standards."

In the minds of many leaders, the destiny of the new nation seemed to hinge on the question of race. White southerners were coming to believe that *only* by protecting slavery could whiteness endure—and with it the fate of the nation. If Africans got their freedom, they would want complete equality. That, in turn, would lead relentlessly toward racial intermixture. One Virginia legislator in 1806 expressed the view of many worried white Americans: emancipation would lead to "a blended and homogenous race." What white man, he asked, "will look forward . . . to that condition of society, in which the two races will be blended together; when the distinctions of colour shall be obliterated; when, like the Egyptians, we shall exhibit a dull and uniform complexion. . . . If [emancipation] proceeds, and they continue to mix with the whites as they have already done, as we daily see, I know not what kind of people the Virginians will be in one hundred years."

In the North similar feelings surfaced about the threat of racial mixing to the new American identity. Barring white-black unions became an obsession among some Philadelphians. By the mid-1790s, the minister of Old Swedes Church refused to marry a black man and the white widow of a sea captain. He was "not willing to have blame from public opinion," he said, for sanctioning mixed marriages. A decade later, a devout Philadelphia Methodist painted a picture of black males swarming over "white women of easy virtue," hell-bent on obtaining white wives and producing "mungrels and mulattoes" so rapidly that "in the course of a few years . . . half the inhabitants of the city will be people of Colour."

Thomas Jefferson's earlier optimism about merging the blood of Indians and American settlers also lost its edge. Especially after acquiring the vast trans-Mississippi empire (the Louisiana Purchase) in 1803 from the French, white Americans launched plans for removing all Indian people living east of the Mississippi to the trackless West. By 1813, Jefferson gloomily told a German confidant that the frontier Indian wars that were a part of the War of 1812 "will oblige us now to pursue them to extermination, or drive them to new seats beyond our reach."

As the new nation's small colleges began to mature, professors began to argue that racial differences could not be overcome. Charles Caldwell, professor of medicine at the University of Pennsylvania, asserted the inherent inferiority of Africans and brooded about the social mixing of naturally superior whites and naturally inferior blacks. According to this doctrine, environmental conditions could never alter the fixed character of separate races.

One of Caldwell's Philadelphia friends epitomized the gradual fading of revolutionary optimism about the possibility of forging a harmonious interracial society in the United States. Tench Coxe—debonair merchant, political leader, and essayist—earlier had been an officer of the Pennsylvania Abolition Society and a believer that, if given equality and opportunity, and if supported by education and religion, freed slaves would gradually advance to the status of whites. By 1820 he had completely reversed his earlier views about black capabilities and the mixing of America's many peoples. In a series of essays, lumping together American Indians and African-Americans as unredeemable, completely alien people, Coxe described them as "uncivilized or wild men, without our moral sense . . . [or] our notions of moral character." Most telling was Coxe's fear of granting equality to African-Americans or Indians, whom he considered incapable of attaining "genuine modern civilization." To free slaves or treat Indians equally, he wrote, would mean "the prostration of everything from the cradle of the infant to the couch of age, the bed of virgin purity, and the half sacred connubial chamber."

RACIALISM IN THE ERA OF REFORM

As the age of Jefferson and Madison gave way to the era of Jackson, the hardening of positions on race was widely noticeable—from the drawing rooms of the upper class to the dockside taverns frequented by the laboring poor. Yet the two visions of America captured in the dreams of "T.T." were still jostling for ascendancy. In the three decades preceding the Civil War, the upper hand steadily went to those who spoke stridently for a white America—a nation ruled by and for whites, a nation where keeping the races separate was the best guarantee of preserving white rule.

The muscular and aggressive America of the antebellum era was showing its growing maturity in a variety of ways. Along with the rapid rise of power-driven factories, the spread of canal and railroad building, and the expansion into the West, American progress was measured by the emergence of men of science. As far as race was concerned, however, these scientists were far from progressive. When they began to seek measurable and inborn race differences in the 1830s, they provided ammunition for the proponents of slavery and undermined the intellectual arguments of universalists. Challenging the belief that all humans were innately equal, they claimed that Africans and Indians were inferior by nature. If this was so, then slavery or extinction was their inevitable fate, and even the best-intentioned people could do nothing to alter it.

The mild Philadelphia doctor Samuel George Morton was foremost among the new scientists of race. For years Morton had been collecting skulls from all over the world. When his skull collection reached 256, he tried an experiment. He poured white pepper seed into each skull, measured carefully the interior volume of each cranium (in cubic inches),

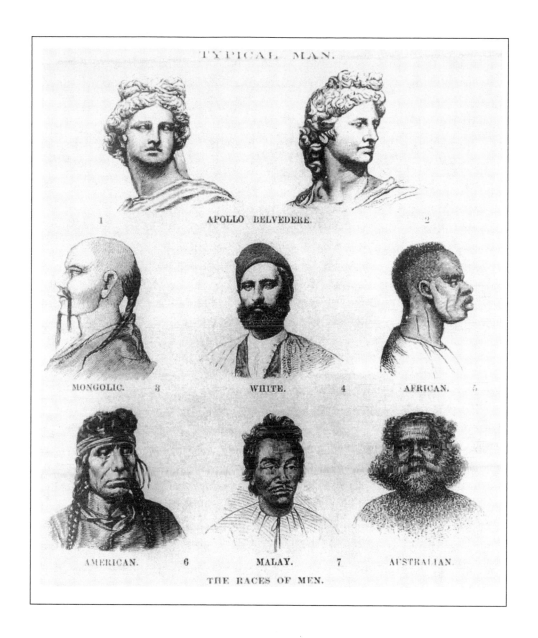

After the Civil War, high school students learned from Arnold Henry Guyot's *Physical Geography* (1866) that the white race was "the normal or typical race" and that all other races were degraded forms of the white race, with their inferiority measured in proportion to their geographic distance from Europe.

processed his data, and then reached his conclusions. The cranial capacity of different races, he announced, varied substantially, and by "reading" these skulls carefully, one could almost explain the rise and fall of nations.

Though the man in the street would not have understood Morton's book *Crania Americana,* he could easily grasp the doctor's main line of argument—that nature, or God, had created distinct branches of the human race and endowed each race differently and unequally. No one could alter these endowments, perhaps unfairly distributed but nonetheless unchangeable. The wise Creator, Morton claimed, had given the Caucasian the largest cranium (the bone cage of the brain). The Mongolian's cranium was next in size, then the Malay's. Next to last in cranium size were American Indians, followed by Africans.

Morton was no apologist for slavery and hardly wished to add to the burdens of free blacks and American Indians. He was a modest Quaker who practiced medicine and taught at the University of Pennsylvania's medical school. As one historian puts it, Morton was "an altogether improbable person to . . . provide the boots and saddles and spurs with which to ride the mass of mankind." But that is what happened. The large skulls of Caucasians, wrote Morton, gave them "decided and unquestionable superiority over all the nations of the earth. . . . In Asia, in Africa, in America, in the torrid and the frigid zones, have not all the other races of men yielded and given place to this one . . . ?"

This was exactly what defenders of slavery and opponents of racial mixing wanted to hear. Objective scientific research, it seemed, had established an ironclad connection between cranium capacity and civilized behavior. In all parts of the country in the 1840s and 1850s, white audiences flocked to hear pseudoscientists called phrenologists explain the human condition. With phrenological charts and casts of skulls in hand, popularizers of Morton's work carried the message from town to town. For a fee they would "read" anyone's head and give advice on one's temperament, marriage prospects, and moral and intellectual potential. Their message was comforting for whites, chilling for Indians and African-Americans.

Far from Philadelphia, in the heart of the Deep South's cotton economy, an Alabama physician gave a twist to Morton's work and greatly popularized it. In *The Types of Mankind* (1854) Josiah Nott promoted the theory of polygenesis. In a book that went through ten editions in fifteen years, Nott argued that, contrary to the biblical account of creation, the different races had separate origins. Blacks and whites, by nature disposed toward different patterns of development, were fated to occupy different stations in life.

Nott had even more ominous ideas. Just as the crossbreeding of animals led to sterile offspring, the mixing of separate races invited disaster. Only pure Caucasian blood could ensure the continuation of civilization. "Wherever in the history of the world the inferior races have been conquered and mixed in with the Caucasian," he warned, "the latter have sunk into barbarism." A population of one hundred white men and one hundred black women, marooned on a deserted island, he asserted, would ultimately become extinct. Similarly, American Indians were doomed to extinction because they were a separate and inferior race.

Polygenecists, who believed that God had created separate species, also concluded that the mixing of races would degrade the superior race and perhaps even destroy it. If racial mixing could be thought of as a violation of the laws of nature, it followed that the offspring of interracial marriages would be biologically defective. Washington Irving, acclaimed novelist of the early nineteenth century, argued that the vast West to which Americans were migrating in huge numbers would become the preserve of "new and mongrel races, like new formations in geology, the amalgamation of the 'debris' and 'abrasions' of former races . . . [descendants of] desperadoes of every class and country yearly ejected from the bosom of society into the wilderness." After retiring as the sixth president of the nation, John Quincy Adams spoke of "how black and white blood cannot be intermingled in marriage without a gross outrage upon the law of Nature."

The white fear of mixing with Indians was not nearly so intense as the fear of mixing with blacks. Nonetheless, it could often be found in the literature of the day. James Fenimore Cooper's famous novel *The Last of the Mohicans* was very popular. In it Americans found confirmation of their views that white women were contaminated by intercourse with Indian men, and that the offspring of these encounters were degenerate mongrels.

In *Legends of Mexico,* another popular novelist, George Lippard, explained to Americans in 1847 that "As the Aztec people crumbled before the Spaniard, so will the mongrel race, moulded of Indian and Spanish blood, melt into, and be ruled by, the Iron Race of the North." By crossing racial boundaries, white Americans debased their blood and became savage Indians. If the white women of the republic mingled with other races, they would produce a polluted generation who could not fulfill America's destiny.

Signifying white America's move toward racial separation, white artists in the 1820s began lampooning free blacks, especially those who had struggled into the middle class. Produced for white consumption, these lithographs provide a telling contrast to the Mexican casta paintings discussed in chapter 3. Whereas the Mexican paintings portrayed Africans, Indians, and mixed-race people seriously and respectfully, the American racial lithographs of the 1830s showed free blacks as illiterate, intemperate, and foolishly pretentious. Such drawings sold briskly enough that Edward Clay, soon to become the premier cartoonist of the Jacksonian period, executed a series of fourteen colored prints entitled *Life in Philadelphia.* They showed hapless former slaves in the northern cities always reaching beyond their abilities and incurably given to malapropisms. In one print, an overweight black man dressed in a cloak covered with Masonic symbols exclaims to a friend: "What 'fect you tink Morgan's deduction [the abduction of William Morgan, who had written an exposé of Masons in New York] gwang to hab on our siety [society] of free masons?" "For honour," answers a second black mason in wing collar, cutaway, and top hat, "I tink he look rader black, 'fraid we lose da 'lection in New York."

With an eye cocked for commercial benefit, publishers picked up Clay's sneering depictions of black middle-class life. They were reproduced in London in 1830 and published in Philadelphia's new *Saturday Evening Post,* soon to become one of the nation's most popular weekly magazines. In Boston, a free black leader complained bitterly that bookstores filled their windows with "cuts and placards descriptive of the negro's deformity" and "the bar-rooms of the most popular public houses in the country sometimes have their ceiling covered with them."

In 1819, David Claypool Johnston of Philadelphia created this lampooning depiction of "A splendid procession of free masons." The black clergyman Absalom Jones, shown in a dignified portrait in the previous chapter, was a leading member of Philadelphia's Black Masonic Lodge. The unknowing viewer of this print could only imagine that Jones, like all free blacks, couldn't spell and dressed pretentiously. Notice the spelling of the "Fre masuns grande loge." [The Library Company of Philadelphia.]

Edward Clay's lithograph series "Life in Philadelphia" mocked whites as well as free African-Americans. But his racist caricatures had the most lasting effects in feeding the growing white sentiment that northern free blacks were a social menace for refusing to stay in subservient roles. [The Library Company of Philadelphia.]

Black minstrelsy, phenomenally popular before the Civil War, allowed white Americans to sort out their views of both free and enslaved African-Americans. Like schoolbooks, minstrel shows branded black Americans as incurably inferior and in fact only a step removed from the animal world. Here the Boston Minstrels offered such songs as "Cudjo's Wild Hunt" and "In de Wild Racoon Track." [The Harvard Theatre Collection, The Houghton Library.]

After the Civil War, blackface minstrel shows had to compete with a new form of entertainment—musical comedies. White minstrels were also challenged by black actors who claimed to be the authentic "delineators of Negro life." But Sprague's Georgia Minstrels kept alive the old stereotypes of inferior and buffoonish black Americans. [The Harvard Theatre Collection, The Houghton Library.]

In creating a ridiculous, mentally crippled black character type for public amusement, white cartoonists also provided raw material for the theater. The buffoonish stock characters created in northern cities for white consumption in the 1830s soon surfaced in minstrelsy. A forerunner of vaudeville, minstrelsy became the runaway best-selling entertainment for rowdy, laboring Americans in the rapidly growing cities. It dominated show business until the 1890s.

Watching white singers and actors who had "blacked up" their faces and hands with burnt cork, the howling audiences by the millions learned to think of black Americans as a separate and vastly inferior branch of humankind. The first full evening of blackface entertainment swept audiences in New York City in 1843—the Virginia Minstrels staging "the oddities, peculiarities, eccentricities, and comicalities of that Sable Genus of Humanity."

Mocking slaves, the minstrel performances contained powerful social and political messages. The minstrels' "coon songs" portrayed enslaved Africans as a happy lot, carefree and contented. Tunes such as "Happy Are We, Darkies So Gay" amounted to a defense of slavery. Stephen Foster's songs—"Oh, Susanna," "My Old Kentucky Home," and "Old Black Joe"—became a staple of minstrel shows. They painted the musical picture of happy slaves, caring masters, and gentle work routines in the fields—the perfect opposite of the hell of slavery that abolitionists described.

Minstrelsy also caricatured free blacks. Speaking in a combination of fractured English and black dialect, the punning white actors ridiculed "bobolashun" (abolition). Minstrels likewise heaped abuse on free black attempts to achieve respectability. By parodying fancy dress, black churches, or even education, the blacked-up white minstrels fed the growing white view that black Americans could never be equal, and *should* never be equal. Minstrelsy, as one historian has put it, "allowed its huge northern white audiences to believe that African Americans were inferior people who did not belong in the North and were happy and secure only on southern plantations."

While most white Americans came to adopt the view that character and culture were literally carried in the genes and that the mixing of races led to polluted blood and impaired intellect, others refused to accept this racial ideology. Largely unnoticed by historians, these people formed families, raised mixed-race children, and strove for a decent place in their communities. For the most part, these Americans issued no tracts, passed no laws, and preached no sermons. Yet they made their ideas, values, and racial openness plain in the way they conducted their lives.

One such couple were William G. Allen and Mary King. Having graduated from Oneida Institute in New York, clerked in a prestigious Boston law firm, and become the first African-American appointed to a professorship at an American college, Allen might have thought he had proven his worth. While teaching at New York Central College in 1851, he became romantically involved with a white minister's daughter, Mary King, who was studying at that interracial school. Allen, the son of a Welsh immigrant father who had married a free mulatto woman, was very light-skinned. Yet to local townspeople, black was black. They threatened to mob Allen and King when it became known that they intended to marry. Driven out of his college position and nearly murdered, Allen arranged to marry his fiancée in New York City. In 1853, they went to England to escape white hostility and to pursue the abolitionist cause.

Even in the Deep South, some men and women challenged the color code. Nathan Sayre, a transplanted New Jerseyan who took up life in Sparta, Georgia, in the early 1830s, was such a person. Establishing himself as a lawyer and a shrewd real estate investor, he became a state's attorney, a member of the Georgia legislature, and a superior court judge. Though never marrying, he sired several children by one of his slave women and later took up life with Susan Hunt, who was herself a mixture of Cherokee, African, and white. For many years they lived together, raising three children in Pomegranate Hall, Sayre's stately mansion in Sparta. Among the volumes Sayre kept in his library was the book by an Englishman, Alexander Walker, titled *Intermarriage; or, The Mode in Which and the Causes Why, Beauty, Health, and Intellect, Result from Certain Unions, and Deformity, Disease, and Insanity, from Others*. It was a rare book for this era, for it argued against the common belief that racial "amalgamation" would inevitably produce degenerate and physically inferior children.

The children of Nathan Sayre and Susan Hunt—dark-haired, dark-eyed, and light-skinned—soon provided evidence that they were anything but inferior. For example, their middle child, known as Cherokee Mariah Lilly, married a white man in about 1853, and her eight children and many grandchildren figured prominently in southern education and reform movements. Among them were Adella Hunt Logan, a graduate of Atlanta University and a leader of the black women's club movement; Henry A. Hunt, Jr., also trained at Atlanta University and later a member of President Franklin D. Roosevelt's "black cabinet"; and Tom Hunt, a graduate of Tuskegee Institute who moved west and served on the agriculture faculty at the University of California at Berkeley.

Other southern white men, including important political leaders, had few compunctions about establishing lasting relationships with black women. The southern social code required that these interracial liaisons, which amounted to parallel marriages, be conducted discreetly. Martin Van Buren's vice president, Richard Mentor Johnson, was a popular Kentucky politician whose devotion to Mary Chinn, his black mistress, and their two daughters caused him no particular difficulties in politics. Sam Houston's friend John Hemphill, who sat as the chief justice of the Texas Supreme Court from 1841 to 1858, lived with his slave Sabina for more than a decade and sent their two daughters to Wilberforce College, an abolitionist training ground in Ohio, for their education.

Giving comfort to those who resisted the growing doctrine of racial separation was a vision of America as a place where all peoples of whatever race would fuse together. In this minority view, such a fusion would not lead to

The sight of black and white abolitionists walking arm in arm through the streets enraged proslavery Philadelphians. Arsonists burned "Pennsylvania Hall" to the ground one day after it opened as a forum for speakers such as William Lloyd Garrison and Sarah and Angelina Grimké. [The Historical Society of Pennsylvania.]

FORBIDDEN LOVE

"mongrelization" and degeneracy but would produce a more vigorous society. To be sure, even most abolitionist reformers were opposed to interracial mixing. Abhorring both slavery *and* African-Americans, many wanted freed slaves removed to Canada, to a separate territory in the vast West, or, ideally, to Africa. However, others in the antislavery crusade, like T.T., whom we met at the beginning of this chapter, had no qualms about racial mixing and upheld the ideal of a biracial democracy. William Lloyd Garrison, the trumpet of abolitionism and racial equality, predicted in 1831 that "the time is assuredly hastening . . . when distinctions of color will be as little consulted as the height and bulk of the body, when colored men shall be found in our legislative halls and stand on perfect equality with whites." Garrison commented to a friend that soon black skin would "no longer be simply endurable, but *popular.*"

In the early 1830s, "amalgamationists" attacked the law in Massachusetts that prohibited interracial marriage. Garrison argued that the 1786 law banning these mixed marriages was "an invasion of one of the inalienable rights of man, namely, 'the pursuit of happiness.' " To take away people's choice of marriage partner was "utterly absurd and preposterous," in his view. "Does a man derive or lose his right to choose his wife from his color?" he asked. "Why, then, let us have a law prohibiting tall people from marrying short ones. . . . Shall fat and lean persons be kept apart by penalties? Or shall we graduate love by feet and inches?" When anti-amalgamationists charged that if Garrison and his like had their way, the country would be swept with black men seeking white wives, Garrison retorted that "the blacks are not so enamored of white skins, as some of our editors imagine. The courtship, the wooing, the embrace, and intermixture—in nine cases out of ten—will be proposed on the part of the whites, and not of the opposite color." David Ruggles, a fearless New York City black activist, agreed. He pointed out acidly that neither he nor "any colored man or woman of [his] acquaintance" was eagerly pursuing cross-race marriage. Expressing a much more modern notion that "black is beautiful," Ruggles maintained that "nothing is more disgusting than to see my race bleached to a pallid and sickly hue by the lust of those cruel and fastidious white men." He pleaded, "To attempt to obstruct the flow of the affections is ridiculous and cruel." Another reformer argued that "when a man and woman want to be married it is *their* business, not mine nor anybody else's. . . . So far from denouncing the marriage of blacks and whites, I would be glad if the banns [announcements] of a hundred thousand such marriages could be published next Sunday."

Massachusetts legislators were unmoved by such published arguments. But by the late 1830s, an avalanche of petitions from whites living in small towns all over the state changed their minds. After viewing ninety-two petitions containing 8,700 signatures in 1843, a large majority of legislators voted to remove the anti-intermarriage law. Although legislators in other northern states would not follow Massachusetts's lead, this was an important blow struck in the name of a person's unqualified right to choose a marriage partner, regardless of popular opinion.

Some of the nation's most important writers kept alive the flame of a polyglot and intermixed America. Herman Melville, in his novel *Redburn* (1849), proclaims, "You can not spill a drop of American blood without spilling the blood of the whole world. . . . On this Western Hemisphere all tribes and people are forming into one federated whole." In another novel Melville's "Confidence Man" asks: "What are you? What am I? Nobody knows who anybody is."

Boston's Ralph Waldo Emerson, the most widely read essayist of the antebellum era, was just as optimistic about a hybrid and "color-blind" people. "A new compound more precious than any," he wrote, is being melded into "an asylum of all nations" where "the energy of the Irish, Germans, Swedes, Poles, & Cossacks, & all the European tribes—of the Africans, of the Polynesians, will construct a new race as vigorous as the new Europe which came out of the smelting pot of the Dark Ages." Wendell Phillips, the thundering abolitionist from Boston, approvingly spoke in 1853 of "The United States of the United Races" and continued to preach this message right into the Civil War years. In 1863 he insisted that the mixing of races was producing a new and vital *genus americanus*. Phillips foresaw "the melting of the Negro into the various races that congregate on the continent" in "gradual and harmonizing union, in honorable marriage. . . . In my nationality," he swore, "there is but one idea—the harmonious and equal mingling of all races. No nation ever became great which was born of one blood."

"The harmonious and equal mingling of all races": this prophecy of Wendell Phillips was made evident in the first half of the nineteenth century by many talented individuals who were the product of interracial marriages. John Brown Russwurm was one. The son of an enslaved African woman in Jamaica and a white father, Russwurm was one of the first black American college graduates in the United States. Founder of *Freedom's Journal,* the nation's first black newspaper, Russwurm went to Liberia in 1829 and became a distinguished leader of the African nation founded by former American slaves.

One can only imagine how accomplished mixed-race leaders in Indian communities must have reacted to the spreading popular wisdom among whites that "amalgamation" produced degeneracy. William Apess, the first American Indian to write extensively in English, was part Pequot and part white. In the 1830s, his was one of the strongest voices to speak out on behalf of Indian rights, and his indictment of white treaty violations and white aggression reached thousands of people.

So, too, many of the most important Cherokee and Creek leaders who were the offspring of mixed-race marriages might have shaken their heads at the pseudoscientific racism sweeping the country. John Ross, principal chief of the Cherokees for nearly forty turbulent years, first married a Cherokee woman, who died on the Trail of Tears in 1839, and then married a white Quaker woman five years later. In the Creek homelands of Georgia and Alabama, two sons born of Creek mothers and Scots-Irish fathers—White Warrior (called William McIntosh by whites) and Red Eagle (called William Weatherford by whites)—were the most important chiefs during the early nineteenth century.

During the Civil War, two "amalgamationist" Indian chiefs, fighting on opposite sides, became generals in the armies of the Union and the Confederacy. Stand Watie, a Cherokee chief, had a white grandparent and married a white woman. Fighting for the South in the Civil War, Watie rose to the rank of general, leading the First Indian Cavalry Brigade. On the other side of that awful bloodletting stood Ely S. Parker, a Seneca who became

Known among his Seneca people as Do-ne-ho-ga-wa, Ely Parker derived his English name from his father, a Seneca chief, who had taken the Parker name from a British officer whom the Seneca had adopted. Though he was trained in law, New York State would not admit Parker to the bar because, as an Indian, he was not a citizen. Native Americans did not gain citizenship until 1924. [The Western Reserve Historical Society, Cleveland, Ohio.]

the military secretary of Ulysses S. Grant and a brigadier general. After marrying a white woman in 1867, Parker became the first Indian to hold the position of Commissioner of Indian Affairs, responsible for Washington's relations with the 300,000 Indians living in the United States.

For white Protestants, who dominated politics, business, and cultural affairs in the mid-nineteenth century, America was a redeemer nation chosen by God to reform the entire world. This sense of mission was as old as the first Puritan settlers in New England, who saw their outpost of Christianity as a saving remnant of corrupted Protestantism and a beacon in the wilderness. Two centuries later, in the decades before the Civil War, Americans were still trying to perfect their society. This perfectionist thrust, however, took many forms. In an age of reform, some pursued a vision of a purely white America in which Indians would become extinct and from which Africans would be returned to their homelands, while new European immigrants—mostly English, Irish, and German—left behind their old ways and adapted to the white American republic. In this godly mission, there was no room for cultural or racial mixing with lesser stocks. Sanctioned by science and medicine, endorsed by powerful politicians, and fortified by popular culture, the hostility to racial intermingling had eclipsed the ideal of a mestizo America as the United States began to unravel over the issue of slavery.

For those who still clung to the ideal of a new mixed-race America, the message of the white purists was bone-chilling. Out of the spotlight and out of favor with the majority, they did their best to build pockets of mixed-race life and conduct themselves as honorably as their situations permitted. Sometimes this required leaving America altogether. In other cases it meant a lifetime of anguish and an uncertain future for their children.

LEMUEL HAYNES:
BLACK PREACHER TO WHITE AMERICA

Among blacks, only ministers were likely to have their portraits painted in antebellum America; Lemuel Haynes was one of them. The descendants of Haynes and his white wife are spread throughout the United States today. [The Huntington Library.]

On the eve of the French and Indian War (1756–1763), an unmarried white woman from a respectable family in West Hartford, Connecticut, gave birth to a dark-skinned baby. The father was a man of "unmingled African extraction." Five months later, the mother gave the little boy up for adoption. A pious Massachusetts farmer took the baby into his family as an indentured servant. The farmer's wife, as the foster child would recount much later in life, "treated me as though I was her own child." Growing up, the boy labored with ax and plow on his master's frontier farm. But he also learned to read. Attending a common school, where he devoured a spelling primer and the Bible in the chimney corner, the growing boy developed a lifelong love of reading and a lifelong devotion to Christianity.

This precocious boy, who was named Lemuel Haynes, would go on to become a noted minister, the first black preacher of the Congregational Church, and the author of many published sermons and tracts. Though not remembered in our history books, he became as much the conscience of the new nation as Ralph Waldo Emerson or William Lloyd Garrison.

After completing his indenture, Haynes enlisted in the militia. He fought as a minuteman in the firefight at Lexington, Massachusetts, in April 1774. He stood in the line of fire in the siege of Boston in 1775. And in 1776 he marched through deep snow to Fort Ticonderoga, where the Americans defeated the British. After the war, recognizing his exceptional talents, several New England pastors arranged private studies for Haynes in Latin and Greek. By 1780, at age twenty-seven, they certified him to preach.

For fifty-three years, Haynes preached to white congregations in Connecticut, Vermont, and New York. In 1804, Middlebury College conferred on him the first honorary degree awarded a black American. Through a long life, Haynes bucked the tide of white prejudice, calling to account those who trumpeted America's greatness but would not extend equal rights to those who were dark-skinned. While white Americans were turning their backs on the revolutionary ideology of natural and inalienable rights, Haynes never ceased preaching that "Liberty is equally as precious to a Black man, as to a white one, and bondage equally as intolerable to the one as it is to the other."

White congregations came to accept Haynes, and so did a young white schoolmistress in Middle Granville, Massachusetts, a little town where he was occupying the pulpit. "Looking to heaven for guidance," wrote Haynes's biographer in 1837, "she was led with a consistent and justifiable delicacy to make him the overture of her heart." Elizabeth Babbit and Lemuel Haynes married and had ten children. One son became a lawyer, another a physician, while others farmed.

When Haynes died at age eighty, in 1833, a fellow pastor eulogized him with a full-scale memoir. Haynes, he wrote, belonged in the company of Africans whose memory had cascaded down through the ages: the Roman warrior Hannibal; the poet Terence; Cyprian, the bishop of Carthage; and Augustine, bishop of Hippo. Haynes, a "sanctified genius," belonged among them, joining a company of Africans whose lives could "hardly fail to mitigate the unreasonable prejudices against the Africans in our land."

BUILDING WALLS

Less than a year after Abraham Lincoln's Emancipation Proclamation, on January 1, 1863, his Democratic Party opponents distributed a "Black Republican Prayer." The bogus prayer ran, in part, "May the blessings of Emancipation extend throughout our unhappy lands, and the illustrious, sweet-scented Sambo nestle in the bosom of every Abolition woman, that she may be quickened by the pure blood of the majestic African, and the Spirit of amalgamation shine forth in all its splendor and glory, that we may become a regenerated nation of half-breeds and mongrels . . . and that we may live in bonds of fraternal love, union, and equality with the Almighty Nigger. . . ."

As the election of 1864 approached, the Democrats played the race card to the hilt. Appealing to widespread white racism, they accused Lincoln's Republican Party of turning the Civil War into a "nigger crusade." In campaign literature labeled "Miscegenation, or the Millennium of Abolitionism," they portrayed white women sitting on the laps of black men, white men with black wives strolling through the park, and intermarried blacks, in fractured English, exulting that they had reached the heaven of social and political equality. Democratic Party newspapers spread word of a

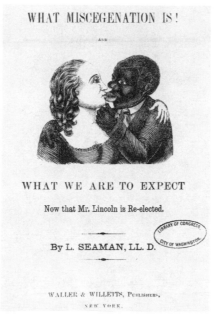

WHAT MISCEGENATION IS!

AND

WHAT WE ARE TO EXPECT

Now that Mr. Lincoln is Re-elected.

By L. SEAMAN, LL. D.

WALLER & WILLETTS, Publishers,
NEW YORK.

This snarling pamphlet was filled with inflammatory charges that those who opposed slavery believed that "Sambo's good time is come—that his millennium is at hand. . . . White men, just stand back and let the conquering heroes pass." The pamphlet may have influenced some voters to vote against Lincoln. But playing the "race card" didn't work because the war itself and economic issues were more important to the average voter. [Library of Congress.]

Republican leader who wanted to "add to emancipation, to confiscation, and to miscegenation, a policy of polygamy" so that "a man could have a yellow wife from China, a brown wife from India, a black wife from Africa, and a white wife from his own country, and so have a variegated family and put a sign over the door: 'United Matrimonial Paint Shop.' "

This race baiting played into anti-black attitudes throughout the North, and particularly among working-class whites. In their attempt to defeat Lincoln in the 1864 election, the Democratic Party deliberately fueled a phony argument over race mixing, which was something most abolitionists actually opposed. Lincoln won, nonetheless. But the wounds opened by such coarse and brutal language ushered in a half-century of bitter racialism. If the tide was running against the dream of a mestizo America in the decades leading up to the Civil War, the half-century after that great carnage saw it nearly drowned forever.

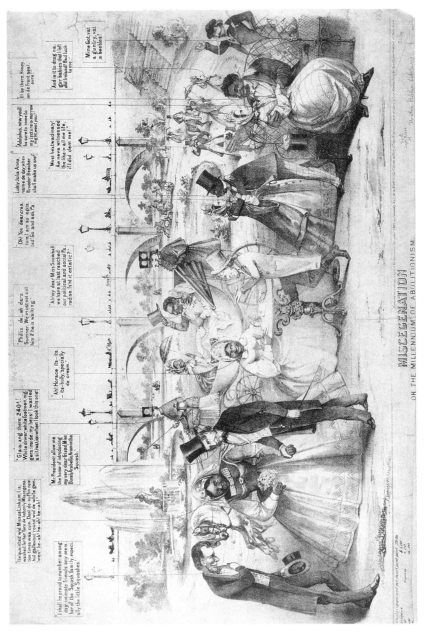

The word "miscegenation" entered the English language at the time this political campaign print appeared in New York City in 1864. In a political pamphlet, two Democratic newspaper journalists blended the Latin *miscere*, "to mix," and *genus*, "race." "It is a war . . . of amalgamation," their pamphlet announced, "a war looking, as its final fruit, to the blending of the white and black . . ." [Library of Congress.]

FORBIDDEN LOVE

THE DREAM DEFERRED

An optimist might have expected otherwise. After all, Lincoln's Emancipation Proclamation and the Thirteenth, Fourteenth, and Fifteenth Amendments to the Constitution freed four million slaves and guaranteed them equal rights as citizens of the United States. The law of the land seemed to be saying that all humans were equally endowed at birth and that all were brothers under the skin.

But that wasn't the reality that people experienced. Not just in the wounded South but also in the victorious North, an obsession with race seized the nation. Freedom for enslaved African-Americans generated a bitter argument about racial characteristics and race relations. Many whites wanted to avoid the issue altogether by sending all blacks, those newly freed and those freed long before, somewhere outside the United States. But this was not really an option. How could white Americans ask blacks to leave the country when African-American soldiers had shed their blood to preserve the Union and their forebears were buried on the American soil they had cultivated for generations?

So the nation worked to bind its wounds. The president and Congress faced a gigantic task of Reconstruction: reunite the warring states; elevate the African-American from slave to citizen; incorporate the black population into American life. For twelve years, from 1865 to 1877, northern Republicans pursued the business of creating a biracial democracy. It was a breathtaking effort to redeem a promise issued a century before in the Declaration of Independence—that all men are created equal. Tragically, the weight of white opinion and the immensity of white power stood in the way. Though they lost the Civil War, white southerners had no intention of surrendering their social, economic, and political power. White northerners were, soon enough, ready to agree. After the end of the North's military occupation of the South, in 1877, the freedmen lost what little they had gained. Even the Freedmen's Bureau, the main instrument for creating racial equality, fell victim to the resurgence of white supremacy.

How did a free democratic society, trying to reestablish its national greatness and proud claim that every person should be judged as an individual, justify the denial of black rights after the failure of Reconstruction? Improbably, an English scientist, roaming the world in pursuit of knowledge about the origins of humankind, provided (unintentionally) a rationale. Three decades before the Civil War, as his ship, H.M.S. *Beagle*, crossed the earth's oceans in search of a complete inventory of the planet's flora and fauna that would enable him to trace the origins of humankind, Charles Darwin provided the perfect scientific "proof" needed by white Americans, both North and South.

On the one hand, Darwin's *On the Origin of Species by Means of Natural Selection, or The Preservation of Favoured Races in the Struggle for Life* (1859) ended the argument between one original creation (monogenesis)

This Democratic Party campaign broadside was produced in Philadelphia to convince voters that the Republicans would tax them silly to support four million emancipated slaves. The freed slave, caricatured as in earlier minstrel shows, lounges while thinking about how the white workingman, in the lower left, chops wood "to keep us children and pay his taxes." [Library of Congress.]

and many creations (polygenesis). His brilliant research made it clear that all humankind had descended from one species and not from several subspecies of humans. This showed, as one white American leader put it, that "the very first step backwards" into the evolutionary past "makes the Negro and the Hottentot our blood relations." Darwin's theories could be used to argue that in the inevitable struggle for survival the fittest prevail and that the more civilized races shouldn't hesitate to eliminate weaker races. "Since we must all die," asked a tough-minded northern Congregational minister, "why should it grieve us that a stock thousands of years behind, in the scale of culture, should die with few and still fewer children to succeed, till finally the whole succession remains in the more cultivated race?" Of course, in this view "the more cultivated race" was the European, and the "stock" that was "thousands of years behind" was the African, soon to be followed into extinction by Indians, Asians, and other inferior races.

Darwin's evolutionary theory seemed to give those who had no intention of extending political equality and economic opportunity to freed slaves all the scientific ammunition they wanted. In the ruthless struggle for survival, the inferior Indians and black Americans could never be truly equal. If they were thousands of years behind the Anglo-Saxon race in evolutionary development, what chance did they have to catch up with the superior Europeans? Doomed by their biological inheritance, black Americans and Indians must accustom themselves to a permanently inferior role while awaiting a lingering racial extinction. The Negro race, declared a white South Carolinian, had "been excluded, as a separate class, from all civilized governments and the family of nations" since it was "doomed by a mysterious and Divine ordination. . . ." Using the language of Darwinian theory, he reminded his generation that both whites and blacks were "distinctly marked by the impress of nature. They are races separate and distinct, the one the highest and noblest type of humanity, the other the lowest and most degraded."

Social Darwinism provided a new "scientific" foundation for race-hate propaganda. Pandering to the white fear that black manhood would express itself in a rush across the color line in pursuit of white women, race propagandists poured out literature that would poison race relations for decades. The argument ran this way: if black freedmen gained political rights and achieved economic independence, they would then demand freedom of sexual choice. In this white nightmare, the end of racial slavery would produce an "unnatural" union between black men and white women. In the South, which had lost 250,000 white men in the Civil War, it might just happen that white women in search of husbands would fall prey to this disastrous passion.

Out of this white fear came the most lurid and hateful literature ever produced in the United States. White writers, northern as well as southern, now scrapped the image of a docile, faithful, amiable slave that they had created in defense of slavery before the Civil War. In its place they depicted a ferocious, avenging black rapist of white women. Hinton Helper, American consul at Buenos Aires after the Civil War, published a widely read diatribe about Negro degeneracy with section titles such as "The Negro's Vile and Vomit-Provoking Stench." Advocating racial extermination for all "swarthy and copper-colored ghouls," he deplored all forms of contact between white and black Americans. New York City's John Van Evrie, a medical doctor, warned that the "negro kissers" in Congress and "the whole gang of Abolition mongrels and traitors who now darken and disgrace the Capitol of our country with their presence, would not change a single iota of his [the black American's] physiognomy from what it was six thousand years ago."

Armed with literature from some of the nation's best educated men, racial extremists in the South worked to preserve their racial caste system with brutal measures that would hold the black male in check. The creation of a rigid color line, one that never existed under slavery, now became essential to them. White masters and overseers, by their easy access to slave women, had blurred racial categories through the long history of slavery. The 1860 census made this quite clear, revealing that approximately one out of every eight black Americans in the South had white ancestors. But after Reconstruction, white southerners separated the races by segregating schools, transportation, and public facilities. Limiting interracial contact, at least between black men and white women, became essential to suppressing the nation's black citizens economically and politically.

The Ku Klux Klan, founded in 1872, used terrorist tactics to institute the new post-slavery, white-supremacist racial order. Using clubs, guns, and the lynch rope to intimidate and repress black southerners, the Klan forced the races apart. From the 1870s through the 1920s, the Klan's fear and hatred of black manhood expressed itself in an orgy of violence. Meanwhile, a torrent of brutal language poured from politicians and presses to justify their vigilante justice. Senator Ben "Pitchfork" Tillman of South Carolina, leader of the southern race extremists, depicted the freedman as "a fiend, a wild beast, seeking whom he may devour." Campaigning for governor of Mississippi in 1900 from an ox drawn lumber wagon, James Vardaman described the black southerner as a "lazy, lying, lustful animal which no conceivable amount of training can transform into a tolerable citizen." The "good darkies" of the slave South, wrote Thomas Nelson Page, one of the nation's most widely read authors, had taken the gift of freedom and transformed themselves into "lazy, thriftless, intemperate, insolent, dishonest [individuals] without the most rudimentary elements of morality." Celebrating the Ku Klux Klan, the Baptist minister and best-selling novelist Thomas Dixon sketched the black rapist for the American public:

> He had the short, heavy-set neck of the lower order of animals. His skin was coal black, his lips so thick that they curled both ways up and down with crooked blood-marks across them. . . . The sinister beady eyes, with brown splotches in their whites, were set wide apart and gleamed ape-like under his scant brows. His enormous cheekbones and jaws seemed to protrude beyond the ears and almost hide them.

In 1915, Dixon's novel *The Clansman* was made into a movie, the epic *Birth of a Nation,* which proved a wildly popular feature. In this movie, D. W. Griffith, the rising-star director of the new Hollywood film industry, gave moviegoers all over the country a riveting tale of white-robed Klansmen bravely trying to restore order and restrain black bestiality in the post–Civil War South. The silent film showed former slaves reveling as members of state legislatures. Their bare feet propped up on desks in leg-

"THE NEGRO A BEAST"

...OR...

"IN THE IMAGE OF GOD"

The Reasoner of the Age, the Revelator of the Century!

The Bible as it is!

The Negro and His Relation to the Human Family!

The Negro a beast, but created with articulate speech,
and hands, that he may be of service to
his master—the White man.

The Negro not the Son of Ham,

Neither can it be proven by the Bible, and the argument of the theologian who would claim such,
melts to mist before the thunderous and
convincing arguments of this
masterful book.

...BY...

CHAS. CARROLL,

Who has spent fifteen years of his life, and $20,000.00
in its compilation.

PUBLISHED BY
AMERICAN BOOK AND BIBLE HOUSE,
ST. LOUIS, MO.
1900.

The Protestant churches were deeply involved in stigmatizing African-Americans and in promoting the idea that freedmen were intent upon marrying white women. The American Book and Bible House published this book by a Protestant minister in 1900. The author argued that interracial marriage was the greatest of all sins and therefore mulatto children did not have "the right to live." [Department of Special Collections, Charles E. Young Research Library, UCLA.]

islative chambers, they swilled liquor from flasks as they passed a law legalizing interracial marriage. In the climactic scene, a white southerner leads a Ku Klux Klan lynch mob after his sister leaps to her death to avoid rape at the hands of a black monster. After lynching the black rapist, the Klan mob saves another white damsel from forced marriage with the mulatto lieutenant governor of a southern state ruled by northern carpetbaggers. President Woodrow Wilson arranged for a special viewing of this chilling movie in the White House.

Black activists cried out against such foul depictions of black men released from slavery as lust-filled rapists of white women. In 1892, Frederick Douglass charged that whites' hysterical campaign against rape of white women by black men (a quite rare occurrence, actually) was raised only "since the Negro has become a citizen and a voter." Ida B. Wells devoted much of her life to exposing how "lynch law" mocked American principles of due process and color-blind justice. She argued that it was white southern fury at "giving the Afro-American his freedom, the ballot box, and the Civil Rights Law" that spawned the ghastly wave of lynching. Black protests against the showing of *Birth of a Nation* met with little success.

The new era of hate-filled race bigotry drastically affected the offspring of interracial marriages. Before Emancipation, enslaved mulatto men and women enjoyed a higher status than blacks in both black and white society. Whites raised no alarm about white blood mixing with black blood as long as it was free white men mingling with enslaved women. Disproportionately, mulattoes became African-American leaders in the free North and the core of the black middle class. But after the Civil War, when hostility to race mixing reached new heights, the status of the mulatto sank swiftly. In books and pamphlets the mulatto was described as syphilitic and physically stunted, immoral and mentally impaired, psychologically tortured about mixed inheritance, and sterile—like the mule, from which the term was derived—beyond the third generation. In short, the mulatto was an offense to nature. An outpouring of purportedly scientific research argued that racial mixing produced sterile and anemic offspring that would lead American society toward a Darwinian fate of racial unfitness. This

A LITERARY DEBATE IN THE DARKTOWN CLUB.
Settling the Question.

Currier and Ives were highly successful publishers of lithographs created to adorn the walls of middle-class homes. Part of their success was in publishing a series of paired lithographs where the pretensions of free black, such as this literary debate, turned into havoc. [Library of Congress.]

A LITERARY DEBATE IN THE DARKTOWN CLUB.
The Question Settled.

huge body of literature undergirded the increasingly harsh racial ideology of the period, strengthening the prejudices of the man in the street by giving them the blessing of academic and scientific authority.

The rise of state laws banning racial intermarriage reflected the growing white abhorrence for race mixing. Devoted to the idea of white purity, lawmakers began to set racial boundaries deemed crucial to the maintenance of an orderly society. In the South, only in the District of Columbia could a person freely choose a marriage partner. In the Midwest, only Ohio and Michigan allowed all people to marry. In the West, only Washington and New Mexico did not prohibit interracial marriage. Most other western states forbade it not only between black and white but also between Asian and white partners. In Oregon and Arizona, marriage between an Indian and a white became illegal as well. All of these laws banning racial intermarriage were designed to control the sexual choices of white women, although they applied equally to any white man who might wish to marry a black, Asian, or Indian woman.

The very definition of "Negro" reflected the shifting white attitudes on race and race mixing. In most southern states before the Civil War, the law defined a Negro as anyone who was at least one-fourth black—that is, with at least one black grandparent. This conferred whiteness on whoever was less than one-quarter black. But by the dawn of the twentieth century, many southern states were redefining "Negro" as anyone who was at least one-eighth or one-sixteenth black. In the final step, accepting the notion that black blood contaminated white blood, lawmakers in several states defined as black anyone with one drop of African blood. In Virginia, for example, the legislature changed the one-fourth rule that had stood since 1787 to one-sixteenth in 1910 (including anyone with one great-great-grandparent who was black), and then adopted a "one drop" law in 1924. In effect, this erased the in-betweenness of mixed-race people. A single drop of ancestral African blood marked a person forever.

The new definitions of whiteness and blackness, the product of congealing white racism, had the effect of driving together the light-skinned African-American elite and the fully black masses. By the early twentieth century, the old division between blacks and mulattoes had waned. Politically astute black leaders understood that unifying African-Americans depended upon this. The father of Atlanta's former mayor Julian Bond, who was three-sixteenths black, three-sixteenths Indian, and ten-sixteenths white, declared "the necessity that all of us black men in America and the world stand together."

While white racism promoted unity among African-Americans of all skin shades, it also fed a growing distaste in black America for racial blending. Particularly, African-Americans opposed the mingling of white men with black women. This seemed all too much like the viciously exploitative system under slavery, when white men wielded a cruel sexual power over enslaved black women. In the early twentieth century, many mixed-blood blacks spoke disparagingly of the white blood in their own veins. On the eve of World War I, Howard University's student body seemed to confirm the growing black aversion to racial intermingling. At most, only 6 of its 1,551 students had a white parent—evidence perhaps of the growing white crusade against "amalgamation," but evidence as well of the distinct preference of black America's most successful families for in-group marriage.

This did not mean that African-Americans had no internal arguments about skin color, marital choices, and self-identity. Color itself, in the post-emancipation generations, continued to be an ever-present topic. With deep roots in the past, arguments surfaced in black newspapers and magazines about skin lighteners, hair straighteners, and other outward aids to beauty and gentility. Whether African-Americans were contending that lighter was better or darker was more beautiful, they used the language of race to describe their identity.

Consciousness of color had been important within black communities for generations. Light-skinned African-Americans, most likely to be freed under slavery and thus forming the free black elite in cities such as Charleston and New Orleans, came to dominate what became known as the "mulatto elite" in cities across the country. Some black colleges, such as Tougaloo and Howard, became strongholds of light-toned African-Americans. The leading black sociologist of the World War I era, E. Franklin Frazier, found a black American society roughly divided into a light-skinned elite, a "brown middle class," and a "black proletariat." In this

Be His Christmas Belle

with Lighter Brighter skin

Be the miss under the mistletoe . . . popular, envied and admired for smoother, softer-looking skin. Use Black and White Bleaching Cream as directed, watch your skin take on lighter, brighter beauty. Its bleaching action works effectively inside your skin. Modern science knows no faster method of lightening skin. Buy it today.

Get Black and White Bleaching Cream at all drug counters, 35¢, 60¢.

BLACK AND WHITE
BLEACHING CREAM

Madame C. J. Walker, the first African-American millionaire, produced creams, oils, and other preparations for lightening skin and straightening hair. Advertisements such as this filled black magazines throughout the twentieth century; this advertisement appeared in *Ebony* in the 1950s.

hierarchy of pigmentation, which whites ignored in favor of treating all black Americans as part of a degraded class, color mattered greatly. For that matter, so did the curl or straightness of one's hair, the thickness or thinness of one's lips, and the narrowness or breadth of one's nose.

The crux of this calculus of color came down to this: descendants of enslaved Africans, inheritors of 300 years of Euro-American racial attitudes, and living in a society where race mattered hugely, gravitated toward an uneasy, and often intensely painful, middle ground where light skin was favored but too light, nearly white, was undesirable. Interviews conducted by several black sociologists after World War I revealed that a majority of black Americans wanted to be light-skinned, to marry other light-skinned people, but never to be considered white or even mingle with whites. The millions of hard-earned dollars spent on hair relaxers and bleaching creams signified the desire not to be white but to be not so dark. The same desire explains the tendency of upwardly striving black men to marry light-skinned African-American women and the common hope of black parents of that era for a lighter-skinned child.

Thousands of other black Americans avoided this painful middle ground, the world of light-skinned African-Americans, by passing into white society or helping their children do so. If one was so light-skinned that nobody would know, far away from one's hometown, that one had a black great-grandmother or great-grandfather, it was possible to escape prejudice and open doors for jobs and social status by pretending to be white. Two of Thomas Jefferson's sons, conceived with his slave Sally Hemings, vanished into white society in the Midwest. One of the third president's grandsons, John Wayles Jefferson, fought in the Civil War as a white lieutenant colonel in the Union Army. Today, after DNA evidence has proven Jefferson's paternity, dozens of "white" descendants from his partnership with Sally Hemings are meeting their long-lost relatives who have darker skin color and have defined themselves as black Americans, but who have always insisted that they were part of Jefferson's family tree.

The number of very light-skinned people who fit the official definition of "Negro" and secretly passed into white society can never be known. But the number was large. The most informed estimate is that about 3,000

Americans each year passed into white society after the Civil War, about 5,000 annually by the turn of the twentieth century, and perhaps 15,000 per year by the 1940s.

THE ASIAN-AMERICAN COMPLICATION

The white fear that the Anglo-Saxon bloodstream would be contaminated by racial intermingling extended to Asian immigrants. Beginning with California's Gold Rush in the late 1840s and continuing through the 1870s, Chinese free immigrants and male contract laborers began to fill the enormous labor needs of an expanding nation. As miners, railroad construction laborers, drainers, ditchers, levee builders, and harvesters, the Chinese made up a quarter of all laborers in California in the 1870s. And of every twenty Chinese immigrants, nineteen were men, which is to say that they came to America without wives or prospects of finding any.

Prized for their labor in the 1850s, the Chinese were detested within a single generation as an alien element that would infect, if not corrupt, white culture. The Chinese, like Africans, declared Henry George, a California political leader, were "an infusible element" of "utter heathens, treacherous, sensual, cowardly and cruel." Hinton Helper, the notorious Negrophobe, lumped Chinese, Indians, and Negroes together. "We should so far yield to the evident designs and purposes of Providence," he wrote, "as to be both willing and anxious to see the negroes, like the Indians and all other effete and dingy-hued races, gradually exterminated from the face of the whole earth." At California's 1878 Constitutional Convention, one delegate borrowed language used on the other side of the continent to condemn black-white marriages as defilement. "Were the Chinese to amalgamate at all with our people," he warned, "it would be the lowest, most vile and degraded of our race, and the result of that amalgamation would be a hybrid of the most despicable, a mongrel of the most detestable [sort] that has ever afflicted the earth."

This racist language legitimized white attacks on Chinatowns up and down the West Coast. Burning, pillaging, and killing in the 1870s and

White businessmen used trade cards such as this to drive Chinese laundry operators out of business. The message here is that patriotic Americans should kick Chinese laundrymen back into the Pacific Ocean. However, many California businessmen welcomed the Chinese as "biped domestic animals in the white man's service . . . the perfect human ox," as one Fresno newspaper put it. [Library of Congress.]

1880s, white Californians obtained the Congressional Exclusion Act of 1882, which closed the door to further Chinese immigration and denied citizenship to immigrants already in the country.

When white hostility turned the valued Chinese levee builder and hard-working transcontinental railroad builder into the despised yellow heathen, the notion of racial mixing became not only undesirable but detestable and dangerous. As early as the 1860s, four western states—Nevada, Oregon, Arizona, and Idaho—banned white-Asian (and white-Indian) marriage. By the turn of the twentieth century, the leader of the American Federation of Labor informed the annual convention that "every incoming coolie . . . means so much more vice and immorality injected into our social life." In a petition to Congress, white San Francisco citizens declared the offspring of marriages between whites and Asians "invariably degenerate." A few years later, in 1901, California banned marriages between whites and Asians.

RACIALISM AT ITS WORST

The rush of states to condemn and criminalize interracial marriage and to redefine degrees of black, white, Indian, and Asian blood tells us how important it was to turn-of-the-century white Americans to keep racially defined groups separate. To racial purists, more precise laws addressing definitions of race by blood proportion were critically important because the courts could not keep separate what they could not categorize. But when states moved from defining white as no less than seven-eighths white, fifteen-sixteenths white, or completely free of even one drop of "black blood," confusion reigned. For example, if a brother and sister who had one great-grandparent who was black lived twenty feet apart, across the Kentucky–North Carolina border, the North Carolina brother would have been legally black with all the disadvantages that carried and the Kentucky sister would have been white with all the advantages that meant. The brother's children would go to black schools, the sister's children to white schools. The North Carolina brother would go to jail for marrying a white woman. The Kentucky sister could marry *only* a white man. North Carolina's one-eighth black blood law and Kentucky's one-sixteenth black blood law made all the difference.

In this early-twentieth-century atmosphere, racial intermingling dropped sharply. Frenzied opposition to racial intermarriage reached its height in the era of World War I, at a time when the United States, under

President Woodrow Wilson, proudly paraded the banner of democracy at home and abroad. This is also the era when the eugenics movement, repeatedly using terms such as "hybrid degeneracy" and "mongrelization" to describe racial mixing, swept the country.

The apostle of the eugenics movement was an eastern establishment lawyer who bore the name of two presidents. Born to a wealthy family in New York City, Madison Grant was educated at Yale and Columbia. His special passion was in preserving the treasures of America: the buffalo, the redwoods, and the white race. In *The Passing of the Great Race,* Grant brought to a fever pitch the white fear that racial intermixing would destroy the intellectual and moral attainments of the white race. The children of mixed unions would inevitably degenerate to the lower type. "The cross between a white man and an Indian is an Indian," he wrote; "the cross between a white man and a negro is a negro; the cross between a white man and a Hindu is a Hindu; and the cross between any of the three European races and a Jew is a Jew."

Grant's ideas about race "mongrelization" were not new, but the remedies he recommended were chillingly so. Admitting that people instinctively indulged "a certain strange attraction for contrasted types," he urged strict enforcement of laws forbidding interracial marriage. Beyond that, he warned that racial purity could be maintained only if whites with deficiencies were sterilized. Defective infants would have to be "eliminated." In short, "The laws of nature," he explained, "require the obliteration of the unfit, and human life is valuable only when it is of use to the community or race." Because "Maudlin sentimentalism" was "sweeping the nation toward a racial abyss," the time had come to scrap the "national motto" of ignoring "distinctions of race, creed or color."

Grant's belief that "the cross between any of the three European races and a Jew is a Jew" speaks to the belief among most white Protestant Americans in the early twentieth century that Jews and other non–Anglo-Saxon immigrants such as Poles, Greeks, and Italians were not really white. Instead, they, too, were separate and inferior races. Racial walls were now constructed to protect the purity of the Anglo-Saxon race from swarthy Southern and Eastern Europeans flooding into the country.

The immense tide of Jewish immigrants from Eastern Europe between 1880 and 1914 fed this view. Some 2.3 million Jews, most of them speaking Yiddish and coming from poor, religious backgrounds, dwarfed the much smaller number of Jews—mostly German—already in the United States. Most of the new immigrants took up life in America in the East Coast cities, especially in New York City. Living in tenements, laboring in sweatshops, and clannishly maintaining their language and culture, they seemed hardly assimilable to most white Protestants. Intermarriage between a Jew and a Protestant became almost as unthinkable as a union between a black and a white American. Though no states passed laws to prohibit intermarriage between Protestants and Jews, Protestants came to think of Jews as a racial as well as a religious group. In the Protestant view, Jewish blood would defile Aryan blood just as surely as black blood would pollute white blood. Jews were as thoroughly and systematically excluded from universities, businesses, and social organizations as black Americans.

By the eve of World War I, white lawmakers, judges, scientists, and popular writers had decided that nearly every aspect of human life could be understood in terms of race. Race determined one's intelligence, morality, character, human worth, and even one's ability to marry successfully and have healthy children. Blood would always tell. Even if they could not define the term "race," most Americans were sure they could categorize the next person they encountered in the street by racial type. Defining and enforcing racial classifications seemed as American as baseball and the movies. Out of such a mind-set came a rising white rage against race mixing, paralleled by the disparagement of mixed-race offspring. Even among black Americans, the feeling grew that race mixing was undesirable, though hardly disastrous. As for Jews, though they hated the way they were stereotyped as unclean, lecherous, loud, and overbearing people, they were not eager to intermarry with Protestants or Catholics. In New York City, the center of American Jewry, fewer than 1 percent of the Jewish immigrants in the early twentieth century married outside their religion. "To our parents," remembered the son of one such Jewish immigrant, "we were always Jews, never American."

EDMONIA LEWIS:
CHIPPEWA–AFRICAN-AMERICAN SCULPTRESS

She was born in 1844 in unfavorable circumstances that gave no hint that she would win renown as an artist. Her father was an African-American manservant; her mother was Chippewa or perhaps half-Chippewa and half-white. Her father seems to have disappeared because when her mother died, Edmonia Lewis at age five went to live with her mother's sisters. While living with them she went by an Indian name, Wildfire, as did her older brother, who was named Sunrise. Poor and orphaned, she fished for food, made moccasins to sell, and lived as a Chippewa. But she also got a bit of schooling in Albany, New York.

Growing up as the nation careened toward civil war, Edmonia showed a special artistic spark that carried her, at the age of fifteen, to Oberlin College, the first American college to admit women and African-Americans. At Oberlin, while learning to draw and paint, a fierce determination to succeed arose in her breast. So did a desire to do her part in the crusading abolitionist ranks to which Oberlin contributed many of its students.

Before finishing her studies at Oberlin, as the Civil War was peaking, Lewis moved to Boston. There she studied with an accomplished sculptor and began to shape clay and plaster medallions of such antislavery heroes as William Lloyd Garrison, John Brown, and Robert Gould Shaw. Her bust of Shaw, the white Boston hero who died leading the black Massachusetts 54th Regiment into battle at Fort Wagner, South Carolina, was such a success that it enabled the twenty-year-old Lewis to move to Rome. There she studied among the world's most promising sculptors. Soon her talents won her mention in guidebooks that brought touring Europeans and Americans to her studio. The first Indian and African-American sculptor to gain an international reputation, she rendered much of her work according to classical conventions that focused on religious figures and national heroes. But Lewis also drew inspiration from her black father and Indian mother, sculpting *Forever Free,* a statue of a slave couple rejoicing in the news of Emancipation; *The Old Arrowmaker and His Daughter,* which drew on her own youthful Chippewa experiences and depicted Native Americans as dignified and proud; and a bust of Richard Allen, Philadelphia's beloved minister of "Mother Bethel," the first African Methodist-Episcopal Church. Lewis's career was crowned in 1876 when millions of visitors to the Philadelphia Centennial Exposition, the one-hundredth birthday of the United States, gazed at her sculpture of a dying Cleopatra. The sculpture caused a sensation. One newspaper at the time said, "*The Death of Cleopatra* excites more admiration and gathers larger crowds around it than any other work of art in the vast collection of Memorial Hall." The half-Chippewa, half-African-American girl had captured the nation's attention.

An American touring Europe after the Civil War might have found his or her way to Edmonia Lewis's studio, for she was listed in the guidebook everyone used for Rome and other cities. Her sculpture *Forever Free* is in the museum of Howard University in Washington, D.C. [Photographs and Prints Division, Schomburg Center for Research in Black Culture, The New York Public Library, Astor, Lenox, and Tilden Foundations; photo of sculpture courtesy Howard University.]

INTERRACIAL RENEGADES

Given the mood of the nation between the Civil War and World War I, one might think that every American would dutifully stick to racial compartments and spurn romance and marriage across the color line. Yet crossing the color line was by no means uncommon. It happened in every part of the country. As rural southern blacks flocked northward to industrial cities, and as smokestack America's throbbing factories brought together laborers from all over the world at the height of immigration between 1880 and 1914, people of all cultural backgrounds defied the official racial dogma. And in every part of the country, old mixed-race communities continued to exist and new ones formed.

ESCAPING BLACKNESS

For some Americans, it was worth hiding one's mixed-race heritage and even blotting from memory one parent or the other in order to escape the racial prejudice that severely hobbled one's chance of succeeding in late-nineteenth-century America. Typically, "passing" into white society was possible for those whose father was white and whose mother was a light-skinned woman born of a master-slave liaison. Such was the case of Michael Healy and his siblings, who used the escape hatch of "passing" to fulfill their potential in a racist society.

According to the white wisdom of his generation, Healy was a degenerate child who should never have been born. Michael's father, Michael Morris Healy, was an Irish immigrant who moved quickly to the Georgia frontier after reaching America in 1815. He prospered there, acquiring land and purchasing slaves. By the late 1820s, he owned thousands of acres and forty-nine slaves. One of them was Eliza Clark, a light-skinned woman who was one-eighth black. In 1829, when she was sixteen, Michael's father took Eliza as his common-law wife. Through twenty years of marriage, broken only by the death of both of them in 1850, they raised ten children. Georgia law prohibited racial intermarriage, so a lifelong partnership had to go unrecognized in the eyes of the law or the church, admissible only in the hearts of the Irish immigrant and his slave partner.

Michael Healy was born a slave, like his nine brothers and sisters, because one's status followed the condition of the mother, and only a special legislative act could free a slave. But his parents had no intention of allowing their children to remain in slavery. As they reached school age, their father sent them, one after the other, far from Georgia—first to Quaker schools in New York and New Jersey and then to Catholic schools in Massachusetts. Though very light-skinned, they were identified as mulatto youths; but gradually, as they became accomplished students in Catholic seminaries, Michael's older brothers began to leave the stigma of color behind. James Augustine Healy, the oldest boy, became a priest at one of Boston's churches and later the Catholic bishop of Portland, Maine. For several years he had to endure the whispered epithet "the nigger bishop," but in time he became so beloved by Maine's Catholics that this was almost forgotten. Another older brother, Alexander Sherwood Healy, became the rector of Boston's Catholic cathedral. A third, Patrick Francis Healy, became a Jesuit and rose in 1873 to the presidency of Georgetown University in Washington, D.C. Two sisters entered Catholic convents. One became the superior of several convents

Few of Boston's African-American citizens were Catholic when James Healy became a priest at Saint James Church. The church, in fact, was overwhelmingly Irish. His name and the success of his Irish-immigrant father might have endeared him to his parishioners, but he had to overcome his suspected African blood. His mother had died in 1850 at about age thirty-seven, and it is unlikely that Healy made mention of her. [Courtesy Archives, Archdiocese of Boston.]

in Canada and the United States. All of them put their mixed racial identity behind them.

Michael Healy, the fifth son, took a different route when he reached the North. An adventurous youth, less bookish than his brothers and sisters, he took to the sea at age sixteen, first shipping out as a cabin boy on a merchant ship bound from Boston to East Asia. Eight years later he enlisted in the U.S. Revenue Service, a predecessor of the Coast Guard. He received an officer's commission in 1865, at age twenty-five.

When the Revenue Service posted Healy to their Arctic fleet in about 1875, he became a living legend. As commander of the *Bear*, the finest icebreaker of the 1880s and 1890s, "Hell Roaring Mike" spent thirty years rescuing icebound sailors in Alaskan waters, enforcing law and order on the nation's last frontier, and defending native people in their scrapes with

FORBIDDEN LOVE

intruding Americans. A New York newspaper claimed he was "a good deal more distinguished . . . in the waters of the far Northwest than any president of the United States or any potentate of Europe. . . . If you should ask in the Arctic Sea, 'Who is the greatest man in America?' the instant answer would be, 'Why, Mike Healy.' "

Like his brothers and sisters, Healy escaped the stigma of race by identifying himself as white. Light skin and favorable circumstances in the North allowed him this possibility. He solidified this claim by marrying Mary Jane Roach, daughter of an Irish immigrant. There was every reason for him to leave his enslaved mother behind and never admit his mixed-race ancestry. He hungered for a career in the U.S. Revenue Service at a time when obtaining an officer's commission was impossible for anyone regarded as black. Nor would he have served his older brothers and sisters as they rose in the Catholic Church by advertising his mother's slave status. Moreover, to draw attention to his own mulatto status would have

A ship's crew in the late nineteenth century was typically international. Notice that sailors on Captain Healy's *Bear* were from many countries. Life at sea involved learning quickly about other cultures, and sailors became informal intercultural mediators. [The Huntington Library.]

Captain Mike "Hell Roaring" Healy had to dress warmly in sealskins or other arctic furs because life at sea in the Alaskan waters was not a bit like Georgia where he was born. [The Huntington Library.]

invited scorn from those subscribing to the scientific and popular opinion held in his era that the children of racial mixing were biologically defective and emotionally maimed. Playing with the cards dealt him at birth, Healy negotiated his way out of the racial corner to which the laws of the nation consigned him.

SECRET BOUNDARY CROSSINGS

For many Americans who could not hide their racial heritage but found love across the color line, a life of anguish awaited them. Most such stories were never told, securely hidden in the family closets of parents who were angered or embarrassed by the marital choices of their sons or daughters. The rare cases that have been documented speak eloquently to the trauma

FORBIDDEN LOVE

caused by the American law of race so harshly perfected in the late nineteenth century. Such is the case of Elizabeth P. Hulme and George Buck.

Elizabeth Hulme was from a long line of English Quakers who had come to America with William Penn in the 1680s. The daughter of one of the leading citizens of Bristol, Pennsylvania, Elizabeth's early life was happy and productive. Attractive and loved, she grew up outside of Philadelphia in circumstances that rarely exposed her to the violence of industrializing America or the corrosive race relations in the post-Reconstruction South. For all the advantages of her upbringing, Elizabeth never married, though she didn't lack for suitors. Then she suddenly died young, at age thirty-five. It was tragic that life had ended so soon for this beautiful woman. But many members of her family refused to attend the funeral, which was held in her father's home on March 9, 1885. As the *New York Times* reported, "the numerous inquiries made as to the reason for the absence of the near relatives brought out a remarkable story."

The "remarkable story" began when Elizabeth Hulme was a young woman, living with her wealthy aunts, on a farm outside Bristol. There she met a handsome man, ten years her senior, who was the manager of the farm. Although they were powerfully attracted to each other, they knew that their love was forbidden. It was not only that she was from a wealthy family and he, orphaned in youth, from a poor family but that George Buck was "a mulatto of a mahogany shade," as the *New York Times* put it.

Obscured from history is how many years Elizabeth Hulme and George Buck hid their love. Neither married, and Elizabeth "went into society rarely," according to the newspaper report, suggesting that she had eyes for no other man but lived in pain with the inadmissibility of her feelings. Then in 1881, when she was thirty-one and he forty-one, they traveled separately to New York City, where they found a clergyman to marry them. Back in Philadelphia, they lived apart, closely guarding their secret. Elizabeth lived with her parents in Bristol, "passing under her maiden name." "Never until the day of her death," reported the *New York Times,* "did [her parents] suspect the relations that existed between their daughter and George Buck."

When Elizabeth fell ill suddenly, she drew up her will, leaving her considerable estate to her husband. After her death, when the will was read, her father "held down his head in shame during the reading and went out of the room a broken man." Family members contested the will on the grounds that it was not legal. Whether they succeeded in denying George Buck the property his wife brought to their marriage is lost to history.

How many Americans lived out such secret lives in the late nineteenth century? We will never know because the arbiters of white culture fiercely condemned interracial marriage as an affront to nature, an insult to family, and a rebuke to the nation itself. But Elizabeth Hulme and George Buck were far from unique.

RADICALISM AND RACE

It is no surprise that in an era of intense racism, racial boundary jumpers were often those who found much wrong with American society and believed that the nation had betrayed its founding principles. Among the most severe critics of the nation's path toward industrial greatness and expansionist empire were labor leaders in the fast-growing cities. Though most union leaders hated "amalgamationism," some forged notable interracial marriages.

Such was the case of Lucia González and Albert Parsons. Born in Buffalo Creek, Texas, in 1853, perhaps as a slave, Lucy González had grandparents who were Creek, Mexican, and African-American. In 1871, she married Albert Parsons, a white southerner who had served in the Civil War as a Confederate scout. One of Parsons's ancestors had arrived on the *Mayflower* in 1620, and another was a Congregationalist minister in New England. As a young man, before the Civil War, Parsons migrated to Waco, Texas. In marrying González, he turned his back on his brother, the editor of a white supremacist newspaper in Texas. At about the same time Albert was marrying Lucy, his brother, William Parsons, was expressing his disgust for "the mongrel results which have so universally attended emancipation and the fraternization of the races throughout the Spanish Republics of the two American continents."

From this interracial marriage came two mixed-race children and one of the most dramatic stories in labor history. Albert Parsons was a Radical Republican during Reconstruction in Texas, defending black rights and thereby earning the hatred of most white Texans. When they moved north to Chicago in 1873, Lucy and Albert joined the Socialist Labor Party. They soon became leading activists in the 1877 railroad strike—the greatest

Lucy Parsons claimed she was born of John Waller, a Creek Indian, and Marie del Gather, a Mexican. However, she was born a slave in Texas, indicating that her mother was part African-American. When she married Albert Parsons at age eighteen, an interracial marriage in Texas was problematic enough that the couple fled to Chicago. [Archives of Labor and Urban Affairs, Wayne State University.]

labor conflict to that moment in American history. By the mid-1880s, they were the most notable radical couple in the city.

Heading up the labor movement's crusade for an eight-hour day, Albert led 80,000 Chicago workers in a march to support a strike in May 1886. Two days later, two unarmed workers were fatally shot in a fight between pickets and strikebreakers at Chicago's McCormick Reaper Works. At a rally in Haymarket Square to protest this, a bomb was thrown without warning, killing a Chicago policeman. Parsons was among eight labor leaders indicted for conspiracy to commit murder. Though the city attorneys produced no evidence, all eight were convicted. Along with three others, Parsons was executed in November 1887.

Undaunted, Lucy Parsons, a spellbinding speaker with flashing eyes and a fiery pen, carried forth the radical labor message for another fifty-five years, until she died in 1942. She and "Mother" Mary Jones were the first two women to join the International Workers of the World, labor's most radical organization. Working for the Chicago Working Women's Union, Lucy Parsons became a legend on the left for her passionate attacks on lynching and her writings on the issues of rape, divorce, and homelessness.

To this day, both African-American and Hispanic-American historians claim Lucy Parsons as their own. In *The Hispanic-American Almanac: A Reference Work on Hispanics in the United States,* she appears as Lucia Parsons González. In *Black Women in America: An Historical Encyclopedia* she is Lucy Parsons. Of course, biologically she was both Latina and African-American. And despite the American system of categorizing everyone as having one—and only one—race, African-American and Hispanic-American historians have given us dual remembrances of this remarkable woman, both groups claiming her as one of their own.

Only the bravest of Asian-American immigrants crossed racial boundaries, but some did. One was Tye Leung, the daughter of Chinese immigrants, who was employed at Angel's Island in San Francisco Bay, where all newcomers arriving from Asia entered the country. There she met Charles Schulze, the son of German immigrants, who was an Angel's Island immigration inspector. Leung had to brave ostracism in the Chinese community, where disapproval of intermarriage was very strong, just as her husband

In marrying Wong Sue Yue, Ella May Clemons was one of the small number of American women who braved ostracism from family and friends to join with an Asian partner. Most Chinese families were also opposed to racial intermarriage. Of the western states, only Washington and Colorado permitted such marriages. [The Society of California Pioneers.]

faced hostility from his own parents. Forbidden to marry in California, the couple went to Washington State to bind their lives together legally. Both lost their civil service jobs at Angel's Island for defying the racial wall built to keep such lovers apart, and both subsequently joined the blue-collar ranks. Charles became a mechanic and Tye a telephone operator.

In still another case, involving one of the most celebrated American figures of nineteenth-century radicalism, Frederick Douglass violated the ultimate taboo—sex between a black man and a white woman. Douglass was the son of a slave woman and a white father whom he never knew. Escaping slavery at twenty, he became a spellbinding orator, the gifted author of a moving and much-read autobiography, and a great abolitionist leader. "No other black before Martin Luther King, Jr.," one historian believes, "was able to appeal to whites on behalf of racial justice and equality with so much force and effect."

While a young man, Douglass married Anne Murray, a free black woman in Baltimore. Two of their sons fought in the Civil War to help obtain freedom for other black Americans. When Anne died, after a marriage of forty-two years, Douglass married Helen Pitts, his white secretary, in 1884. He honored his mother's people, he explained, in his first marriage, and he honored his father's people in his second. Douglass suffered much criticism from both whites and blacks. Even members of his own family ostracized Douglass and Helen Pitts during a marriage cut short only by his death in 1895.

THE SPORTING LIFE

Of all interracial liaisons, ones involving sports heroes have attracted the most media attention. This was the case in the early twentieth century, when the world's best boxer ruled the headlines and in the process touched the raw racial nerves of whites so forcefully that many legislators tried to pass a national law to ban all interracial marriage. Jack Johnson, son of an ex-slave, became the most stylish and powerful heavyweight in the world. In 1910, when he defeated Jim Jeffries, the best white fighter in the world,

Irene Marie Pineau, like Jack Johnson's previous two wives, was white, beautiful, and willing to endure the taunts of rabid "anti-amalgamationists." [United Press International.]

Johnson became a hero to the black community. Johnson now crystallized the white fear of black masculinity and physical superiority. "That Mr. Johnson should so lightly and carelessly punch the head off Mr. Jeffries," said one New York newspaper, "must have come as a shock to every devoted believer in the supremacy of the Anglo-Saxon race." The search began for a "great white hope" who could wipe the broad smile off Johnson's face and bring him to the canvas.

Even more disturbing to whites than his boxing superiority was Johnson's flouting of racial taboos and his utter disregard for the social rules constructed to govern black behavior. By 1910, Johnson was touring with vaudeville shows, living lavishly in Chicago, driving racing cars, and flaunting his attractiveness to a variety of white women. The "baddest dude" of the day confirmed all the nightmares of white Americans. He crossed the racial boundary to marry the beautiful Etta Terry Duryea in 1911. After her suicide a year later Johnson married Lucille Cameron, another white woman. Outraged, ten midwestern states debated antimiscegenation laws and furious white congressmen introduced dozens of such bills in Washington. None of the national bills passed, but all of them reflected the white rage over a proud black boxer whom women—including white women—found irresistible.

MIXED-RACE COMMUNITIES

While couples such as Albert and Lucy Parsons, Tye and Charles Schulze, and Frederick and Helen Douglass kept aflame the torch of a mixed-race America, entire groups lived in mixed-race communities. Learning to mingle peacefully began in the late teenage years of a small number of young Americans who attended colleges specifically founded as interracial institutions. The most notable of them were Oberlin College in Ohio and Oneida Institute in New York, both established by radical abolitionists in the 1830s.

Neither school began experiments in interracial living without a fight. In 1835, when he heard that brand-new Oberlin was to be integrated, New

Though his own children were opposed to his marriage to a white woman after his wife of forty-two years died, Douglass gained acceptance—and high office such as minister to Haiti—in Washington. He insisted that only by transcending race and embracing a composite nationality could Americans live up to their democratic and egalitarian principles. [Photographs and Prints Division, Schomburg Center for Research in Black Culture, The New York Public Library, Astor, Lenox, and Tilden Foundations.]

England's financial agent warned that "to place black and white together on precisely the same standing will not most certainly be endured," and he predicted that Oberlin "will be blown sky high" if "the darkies begin to come in in any considerable number, unless they are completely separated . . . so as to veto the notion of amalgamation." But generations of Oberlin students, including one of Frederick Douglass's daughters, learned that prejudice dissolved when people studied together, ate together, lived together, and learned together.

At Oneida Institute, the same was true. One white student (for whom Grinnell College was later named) described the student body he found when he entered Oneida: "a motley company of emancipators' boys from Cuba; mulattoes; a Spanish student; an Indian named Kunkapot; black men who had served as sailors, or as city hackmen, also the purest Africans escaped from slavery; sons of American radicals, Bible students scanning Hebrew verse with ease, in the place of Latin odes; enthusiasts, plowboys and printers." Oneida produced many of the African-American leaders of the nineteenth century and fulfilled the dream of its founder, Beriah Green, who wrote that "the red sons of the Western forest, the sable sons of the sunny South have here found a home together, and . . . have lived in peace and love with their pale-faced and blue-eyed brethren."

Farther west, mixed-race communities defied the notion that racial amalgamation would be America's downfall. In the 1880s, when the traveler William Barrows passed through the old beaver-trapping country in Montana and Wyoming, he found towns inhabited almost entirely by people who were thoroughly mixed—French, Indian, English, and Spanish. Impressed by the "color blindness" of these northern Rockies people, Barrows hoped that "we are building a nation, not only in a new world, and under a new system of government, but with a new people. . . . We are no longer English; that expresses but one of our polygenous ingredients. We are Americans." If Barrows had traveled in the Southwest, especially in New Mexico, he would have found similar communities predominately populated by people of Mexican-Indian descent. To this day, the New Mexico highlands are dotted with towns inhabited mainly by Indian-Mexican families, celebrated in such novels as John Nichols's *The Milagro Beanfield War* (1974).

The Sikh immigrants to California in the early twentieth century tell a story of a new combination of previously unacquainted people. When new laws in 1882 excluded Chinese immigrants and in 1907 banned Japanese as well, California's cotton, fruit, and vegetable growers turned to Korea, the Philippines, and South Asia for labor. Among these immigrants were nearly 7,000 Sikhs from the Punjab. Arriving as single men, the Punjabis were socially stranded. They could not bring Sikh women with them, and California's 1901 law prohibited marriage between a white person and a "Negro, Mulatto, or Mongolian." But by the end of World War I, the Sikhs were finding that California's county clerks would issue marriage licenses to people of different races as long as their skin color seemed reasonably close. It was this looseness in the application of the law that soon led to marriages between Punjabi men and Mexican women. "Cotton was the crop that brought most [mixed] couples together," says the historian who has studied this type of interraciality. The Mexican Revolution of 1911 propelled Mexicans across the border into U.S. cotton fields from Texas to California, and there the women found Punjabi, Korean, and Filipino partners.

Between 1913 and 1948 (the latter date marks the overturning of California's law prohibiting racial intermarriage), 80 percent of the East Indian men in California married Mexican women. To this day, several thousand of the children and grandchildren of these Punjabi-Hispanic marriages can be found in every Imperial and San Joaquin valley town. Many of the families can still be found under the name of Singh—the most common Sikh surname—but most have Hispanic first names. The Sikh immigrants built temples all over California's agricultural valleys where the families of Jesus Singh or Alejandro Singh worshiped and married. Finding loopholes in the ruling system of racial division and classification, those who picked the fruit and vegetables served on dinner tables all over the country brought new life to the old dream of a mestizo America.

TEARING WALLS DOWN

She was a graduate of public schools in the North Beach district of San Francisco when she went to Stanford to major in history with minors in sociology and education. Popular and talented, she thrived in her undergraduate years. He distinguished himself academically, studying law and history at Stanford after completing an undergraduate degree at the University of the Pacific. A great favorite among his fellow students at Stanford, he served as president of the debating society. In 1922, when she published her account of their unusual married life in the *San Francisco Bulletin,* she related how they "were attracted to each other at the first." Then she realized gradually "that there was something deeper and broader about him. He seemed to have the education of two men. Although his well-stored mind was exceptionally keen, he was humble and retiring in disposition and I became enamored with his visions of service."

When he proposed marriage just before her Stanford graduation, she began "three terrible months" when a "struggle raged within my locked breast, for there was none but the Almighty in whom I could confide." Her parents would oppose the marriage. "Public opinion would condemn the nuptials and prophesy divorce and other horrors." But finally she concluded that no "member of the human family" should "regard himself as superior to another no matter what the race or the color of the skin. . . . The Scripture verse: 'Man looketh upon the outward appearance but God looketh upon the heart' sang itself into my heart." She realized that she loved this man "to the exclusion of all others and that it would be cowardly for me to break his heart and blight his future because I feared to face popular opinion."

And so Emma Ellen Howse and Walter Ngong Fong were married on June 19, 1897, in Denver, Colorado, where interracial marriage was still permitted. The couple soon returned to California, where Walter practiced international law in San Francisco and became the first Chinese instructor at the University of California at Berkeley. Then he accepted the pastorship of the Chinese Methodist Episcopal Mission in Oakland and also became the head of an organization of educated Chinese bent on overthrowing the Chinese dynasty and transforming the huge nation into a republic. Later, Fong went on to become the founding president of a college in Hong Kong that trained young men in Western ways. Two sons came from this marriage. After Walter Fong's death, Emma Howse Fong remarried, this time to Professor Yoshi S. Kuno, Berkeley's first Japanese instructor.

In 1922, running Emma Fong Kuno's life stories under the titillating title "My Oriental Husbands," the *San Francisco Bulletin* appealed to its readers' fascination with sex between "whites" and "Orientals." But in an editorial published the day after Emma Fong Kuno's last chapter appeared, the *Bulletin* revealed a deeper interest in her story. Asserting that Mrs. Kuno's model marriages were "an exception to the general rule that such alliances commonly end in disappointment, disillusion, and wreck," the editorial strongly advised that "Japanese and Americans should not intermarry." Readers were urged to ponder the views of Herbert Spencer, the popularizer of the Darwinian "survival of the fittest" doctrine, that the mating of "two widely divergent varieties" will produce children of "a chaotic constitution." If people insisted on intermarrying, as the *Bulletin* feared was the case in San Francisco, then "immense social mischief must arise, and eventually social disorganization." Reflecting the view of the white eugenicists, the *Bulletin* urged strict immigration laws that would

THE SHAME OF AMERICA

Do you know that the United States is the Only Land on Earth where human beings are BURNED AT THE STAKE?

In Four Years 1918-1921, Twenty-Eight People were publicly
BURNED BY AMERICAN MOBS

3436 People Lynched, 1889-1921

For What Crimes Have Mobs Nullified Government and Inflicted the Death Penalty?

Is Rape the "Cause" of Lynching?

83 WOMEN HAVE BEEN LYNCHED IN THE UNITED STATES

AND THE LYNCHERS GO UNPUNISHED

THE REMEDY

The Dyer Anti-Lynching Bill Is Now Before the United States Senate

THE DYER ANTI-LYNCHING BILL IS NOW BEFORE THE SENATE
TELEGRAPH YOUR SENATORS TODAY YOU WANT IT ENACTED

NATIONAL ASSOCIATION FOR THE ADVANCEMENT OF COLORED PEOPLE

In 1905 a sociologist observed that "our country's national crime is lynching." In Georgia alone by that time, whites had lynched nearly 500 black Americans. Deep at the roots of white mob violence against blacks was fear mixed with fantasy about the black man as a rapist.

keep white America pure. The "experience and testimony of the author of 'My Oriental Husbands' " must simply be regarded as an aberration.

In the aftermath of World War I, the apostles of racial purity and white supremacy were firmly in command of the nation's destiny. Congress passed a series of immigration laws in the 1920s that slammed shut the "golden door" through which so many millions had passed. The Ku Klux Klan attracted millions of recruits in the North, Midwest, and West, turning the old southern hate group into a national organization stressing Aryan supremacy and controlling local politics from Anaheim, California, to Indianapolis, Indiana. Anti-Semitism intensified as the pre–World War I Jewish immigrants from Eastern Europe pushed their way up the social ladder, meeting resistance along the way from those who prized them only as cheap laborers and not as social equals or economic competitors. Even one of the nation's best-selling novelists, Kenneth Roberts, advised in 1922 that "Any promiscuous crossing of breeds invariably produces mongrels, whether the crossing occurs in dogs or in humans, and whether it takes place in the Valley of the Nile or on the Arctic plain or in the shadow of Rome's seven hills or along the stern and rock-bound shores of New England."

Yet cracks in the façade of Anglo-American Protestant culture were also beginning to show. On the one hand, a group of writers and pioneering social scientists challenged the eugenicists and racialists head-on. At the same time, in major cities, pockets of interracialism developed where writers, musicians, and artists conducted experiments across racial lines that began to carry popular culture in exactly the opposite direction of Madison Grant, Thomas Dixon, and Kenneth Roberts.

CHICAGO

On Chicago's South Side, where the black migrants from the Black Belt cotton South dreamed of a better future, blues and jazz assaulted middle-class white values and took young people by storm. Ministers and "respectable" opinion makers of the metropolis attacked jazz as sensuous and barbaric "jungle music" that affronted dignity and decorum, even destroyed order. But young white musicians, captivated by the freedom to escape the discipline of classical music, joyfully drank in the music of black blues singers and jazzmen in smoky, boozy clubs. White musicians such as Eddie Condon, Benny Goodman, Gene Krupa, Jimmy McPartland, and Milton "Mezz" Mezzrow thrilled to the music of black pioneers of Chicago-style jazz—Joe Oliver, Louis Armstrong, Jimmie Noone, and Johnny Dodds among them. The freedom to express themselves creatively in music brought white musicians together with blacks with whom they had never before mingled. The young Hoagy Carmichael called black jazz a rebellion against "the accepted, the proper and the old. . . . Jazz said what we wanted to say though what that was we might not know." "Mezz" Mezzrow called white jazz musician devotees "teenage refugees from the sunny suburbs" and saw their attempts to emulate the black jazzmen as "a collectively improvised nose-thumbing at all pillars of all communities, one big syncopated Bronx cheer for the righteous squares everywhere."

At first, white and black jazz bands played separately, though their audiences were often mixed. By the 1930s, black vibraphonist Lionel Hampton was playing with white clarinetist Benny Goodman. This was a small step toward breaking down the separation of races, but it was a deeply significant one, for jazz was becoming dizzyingly popular, in Europe as well as America. Jazz clubs were becoming vibrant sites of racial blurring where migrants from the black South and the children of immigrants from Jewish and Italian Europe were turning the music into a mass commercial success. For a generation of young white Americans, black music was America's gift to the world. White jazzman Eddie Condon remembered that in Chicago, white youngsters treated jazz "as if it were a new religion just come from Jerusalem."

On the North Side of the same city, the University of Chicago attracted a new generation of social scientists who set out to recover America's deep multicultural and intercultural past. A band of bright, young sociologists began analyzing the experiences of Polish peasant immigrants to Chicago, southern black tenant farmers, and "Oriental" immigrants to the American

Edward "Duke" Ellington (seated at the piano) was one of the foremost American composers of the twentieth century. His band, soon to become famous worldwide, debuted in 1927 at Harlem's Cotton Club, an all-white nightclub of the "roaring twenties." Millions of Americans who thoroughly disapproved of interracial marriage thoroughly enjoyed interracial music. [Photographs and Prints Division, Schomburg Center for Research in Black Culture, The New York Public Library, Astor, Lenox, and Tilden Foundations.]

West. From these landmark studies came new ways of thinking about race and ethnic relations and intermarriage.

The Chicago academics, led by Robert Park, who had served as Booker T. Washington's press secretary at Tuskegee Institute, mapped out what they believed were nearly universal stages of interaction between different groups. When either Polish immigrants met native-born white Americans or southern African-Americans released from slavery encountered northern whites, four phases of interaction occurred. When contrasting groups confronted each other, the "natural process" began with competition, then came conflict, next they reached accommodation, and finally they blended together. The mingling of people throughout history around the globe proved this pattern, argued the sociologists. Race mixing was not a disaster to be avoided but rather a natural outcome of interracial contact that would be disastrous to resist.

University of Chicago sociologists also undertook a massive survey of race relations on the West Coast in the 1920s. Because they regarded interracial marriage as the focal point of all race relations, they constructed the first questionnaire ever put before these intrepid Asian-white couples who had braved intense prejudice and often skirted the law to make their lives together. Sociologists fanned out, clipboard in hand, to find interracial couples and get their responses to such questions as: "What kind of Oriental man does the American woman marry?" "What seems to be the basis of the physical attraction?" "Are the Oriental men who have married American women of a gay and open disposition or are they steady and reserved?" "How did her family [the American woman's] react to the news that she was going to marry an Oriental?" "Did their feelings alter with time?" "Do they talk about it with their friends?"

Park's race-relations surveys were an attempt to moderate the anti-black, anti-Chinese, and anti-Japanese race riots that were scorching cities all over the country. Whereas in the nineteenth century, cranial measurements and Darwin's theory of the survival of the fittest seemed to favor racialist theories, now the finest social scientists of the day were challenging prejudice and reshaping how America saw itself. Partly in response to the work of Park and other sociologists at the University of Chicago, some colleges launched courses on race relations in the 1920s.

Park and his colleagues brought to Chicago another man who was much ahead of his time on matters of racial fusion. This was José Vasconcelos, a Mexican political reformer during the period of the Mexican Revolution as well as a philosopher, essayist, and an outspoken critic of the United States. Vasconcelos lectured at the university for several years in the mid-1920s, and his message was aimed like an arrow at the heart of the popular eugenicist theories about the dangers of race mixing. Vasconcelos insisted in his lectures to undergraduates that "hybridism in man as well as in plants tends to produce better types and tends to rejuvenate those types that have become static." While white American race-mongers were preaching racial purity, Vasconcelos was predicting that the United States would fail as long as it relegated African and Asian people to inferior positions. Their lack of tolerance and sympathy would be self-defeating because they could not abide a "cordial fusion" of the many peoples of America. "The future race, the definitive race, the synthetical race, the integral race," cautioned Vasconcelos, "[will] be made up of the genius and the blood of all peoples and, for that reason, more capable of free brotherhood and of a truly universal vision."

GREENWICH VILLAGE

A second catch-basin of cultural nonconformists that celebrated interracialism was Greenwich Village in New York City. The unofficial capital of American bohemia, the Village vibrated with artists, playwrights, suffragists, poets, social workers, dancers, photographers, radical students and workers, writers, and musicians—all bound together by reformist politics, sexual liberation, and an intoxicating vision of a multicultural, racially mixed America. If the tide of Klanism, restrictive immigration laws, and race riots were pulling America in one direction, Greenwich Village was hauling America in another. Nothing was off-limits in the Village, whether sexual, political, or artistic. Indeed, the Village was devoted to boundary breaking. Much of America deplored it, but few Americans ignored it.

One of the Village's clarion voices belonged to a brilliant young man of letters whose hunchbacked and deformed body contained a gigantic mind. Though thoroughly upper class and Protestant in background, Randolph Bourne preached that America would never achieve greatness by washing out of its immigrant masses all of their traditions and heritage.

Bourne was fighting an Anglo-Saxon racism that was nearly as cruel in its depiction of Southern and Eastern European immigrants as it was of African-Americans and Asians. The leading sociologist of the day, E. A. Ross, cautioned whites of Northern European ancestry to "Observe immigrants not as they come travel-wan up the gang-plank, nor as they issue

A leading entertainer in the heyday of the Harlem Renaissance, Ethel Waters helped shape an interracial American musical tradition. Millions of Americans flocked to see this jazz and blues singer after she began appearing in the late 1920s in Broadway musicals such as the *Blackbirds* show of 1930 and *Rhapsody in Black*. She received the 1949 Academy Award nomination for Best Supporting Actress in *Pinky,* one of Hollywood's first ventures into interracial plots. [Frank Driggs Collection.]

toil-begrimed from the pit's mouth or mill gate, but in their gatherings, washed, combed, and in their Sunday best. You are struck . . . that from ten to twenty per cent are hirsute [hairy], low-browed, big-faced persons of obviously low mentality. Not that they suggest evil. They simply look out of place in black clothes and stiff collars, since clearly they belong in skins, in wattled huts at the close of the Great Ice Age." These were the immigrants who were to be washed clean in the melting pot. But Bourne had a different vision: "We have all unawares," he said, "been building up the first international nation."

As World War I raged, Randolph Bourne was already celebrating a new kind of American society. This "transnationality," he wrote, would be "a weaving back and forth, with the other lands, of many threads of all sizes and colors. Any movement which attempts to thwart this weaving, or to dye the fabric any one color, or disentangle the threads of the strands, is false to this cosmopolitan vision."

Bourne was an extraordinary thinker and writer in an era when race relations reached their lowest point in American history. He burned with conviction that the white obsession with racial purity should not be allowed to drain the essence out of the varied American peoples. The modern American identity could never be reduced to a single lineage. Instead, Americans had to be repeatedly reforged and refashioned, as people of different backgrounds, ancestral roots, cultural leanings, and skin colors came into contact with each other, both inside and outside marriage.

Though he didn't live in Greenwich Village, the German immigrant Franz Boas became one of its intellectual godfathers. Teaching anthropology uptown, at Columbia University, Boas argued that the common understanding of race made no biological sense at all. Scientists had never agreed on whether there were five, ten, or perhaps forty-five races. Nor could they agree on what markers—skin color, hair type, or blood—best indicated race. Race did *not* determine language, intelligence, character, or customs. If there were such things as mixed-race "degeneracy" and "mongrelization," they would occur in a child whose father had straight hair and whose mother had curly hair as readily as in a child with a Nigerian father and Swedish mother.

Teaching courses on "The Negro Question" and "The Race Problem in the United States," Boas battered down all the old arguments about Negro inferiority. He counseled that the race problem in the United States would be solved only through extensive racial intermarriage. Crossing racial boundaries and producing mixed-race children was "the greatest hope for the immediate future." Consciousness of race, and the vicious white prejudice and discrimination it produced, would slowly dissolve as Indians, African-Americans, and Asian-Americans lost their physical markers—skin color foremost among them.

As new ideas trickled down from leading professors such as Boas and Park, pseudoscientific race-based arguments began to lose respectability. Boas and his academic sympathizers were equally important for listening for all the voices of America. Seeing black prison chain gangs, down-and-out mariners, impoverished Appalachian whites, and every other isolated and dispossessed pocket of Americans as part of an extraordinary mosaic, Boas dispatched his students to every region of the nation. Taking down the life stories and trickster tales related by elderly ex-slaves; tape recording sea chanteys, camp hollers, and prison songs; studying the designs of Navajo weavers and Hopi silversmiths; and listening to cowboy songs and frontier ballads, they captured America's rich and multiracial heritage. Nearly every American songbook or story collection in any school library is sure to have words or music that Boas and his students saved from oblivion.

On the stage in New York, audiences witnessed dance as they had never seen it before the innovative choreographer Martha Graham arrived on the scene. Graham studied the dances of American Indians and other groups. In them she felt the life forces that varied from group to group but always truly represented people's cultural integrity. White Americans visiting the Southwest had seen Hopi or Zuni dances, but never until Martha Graham's dance troupe flew onto the stage had audiences seen a multiracial cast of performers.

One of the Village's most haunted figures even dared to bring forbidden interracial love to the New York stage. Eugene O'Neill's *All God's*

Chillun Got Wings (1924) was a drama of miscegenation, in which a young white woman falls in love with an older black man. O'Neill's plan was to have Mary Blair, the female lead, kiss the hand of her black lover, played by the ruggedly handsome Paul Robeson. Even before the play opened, however, protectors of the color line predicted riots if the scene occurred, even if O'Neill portrayed the white heroine as going crazy before demonstrating her affection. Nonetheless, the show opened—the first of many interracial casts to play to mostly white audiences in the next few decades.

BLACK HARLEM

One hundred blocks north of Greenwich Village an even more important site of cultural ferment was breaking down the walls of racial separation in the 1920s and 1930s. A generation of black writers, artists, dancers, and musicians soon took the nation by storm. Fueled by the great migration of southern blacks to northern cities, self-confident African-Americans wrote about themselves and uncovered a strong and deep tradition tracing back to Mother Africa that shaped a uniquely American black experience.

Not all of the artists of the Harlem Renaissance were political. Still, jazz pianists, composers, and dancers captivated white audiences in musical revues that presented an image of black Americans sharply different from the nineteenth-century minstrel shows. James "Eubie" Blake and Noble Sissle's *Shuffle Along* (1921) and *The Chocolate Dandies* (1924) played to millions of Americans, as well as to Europeans in tours through France and England. *Shuffle Along* paved the way in New York for black musical revues that made household names out of talented young black artists: Josephine Baker, who was introduced in *Chocolate Dandies;* Florence Mills, who starred in *Dixie to Broadway* (1924) and enthralled audiences on both sides of the Atlantic with her singing and dancing; Ethel Waters in *Africana* (1927) and *Blackbirds* (1930); and Bill "Bojangles" Robinson, a singer-dancer with spectacular footwork that Americans would see far more of when he was Shirley Temple's dance partner in later movies.

The young, dapper Langston Hughes, shown here, was the grandson of radical abolitionists, including one who joined John Brown's band that attacked the federal arsenal at Harpers Ferry. Like many of the Harlem Renaissance figures, Hughes traveled to Paris in search of the vaunted color-blind France that had welcomed African-American soldiers in World War I. [Photographs and Prints Division, Schomburg Center for Research in Black Culture, The New York Public Library, Astor, Lenox, and Tilden Foundations.]

White Americans—and of course black Americans as well—loved the black musical revues. One can almost feel the uncoiling of the racist springs that ruled America in previous decades. New York's *Herald Tribune* in its review of *Chocolate Dandies* rhapsodized that "in this cosmopolitan city, and this heterogeneous nation, what can be more to the taste of New Yorkers than the productions such as the American Negro, with all his versatility and innate music, can present?"

Offstage, African-Americans who were writers rather than musicians and dancers had a different effect. Expressing their own identity and venting their anger at American racism, the race-proud men and women of the Harlem Renaissance reached a considerable portion of white America with their writings. Langston Hughes, descended from prominent black abolitionists, used jazz and blues themes and rhythms in his poetry. In one of his bittersweet poems, "America Will Be," he wrote: "O yes, I say it plain, / America never was America to me, / And yet I swear this oath— / America will be."

Many other writers exposed the dark side of America's democracy with a vengeance. Claude McKay's *Harlem Shadows* (1922) contained poems with bitter defiance that shocked many whites: "If We Must Die," "To the White Fiends," and "The Lynching." In 1929, Walter White's *Rope and Faggot: A Biography of Judge Lynch* exposed the grisly vigilante justice dispensed by whites against blacks; white America stood by watching as its basic principles of justice were ripped to tatters. James Weldon Johnson's *Saint Peter Relates an Incident of the Resurrection Day* (1930) indignantly indicted discrimination against African-American mothers who had lost sons in World War I. The poet Arna Bontemps left some readers squirming with his "A Black Man Talks of Reaping":

> I have sown beside all waters in my day.
> I planted deep, within my heart the fear
> That wind or fowl would take the grain away.
> I planted safe against this stark, lean year.
>
> I scattered seed enough to plant the land
> In rows from Canada to Mexico
> But for my reaping only what the hand
> Can hold at once is all that I can show.
>
> Yet what I sowed and what the orchard yields
> My brother's sons are gathering stalk and root,
> Small wonder then my children glean in fields
> They have not sown, and feed on bitter fruit.

As race-conscious as they were, many of the artists and writers of the Harlem Renaissance had close ties with white patrons, some were interracially married, and a few wrote about mixed-race people. One of the latter was Jean Toomer. A light-skinned African-American novelist whose lyrical *Cane* (1923) catapulted him to prominence, Toomer twice married white women. In a long poem, "Blue Meridian" (1936), he saw the solution to the race problem through the creation of a new branch of humankind—the blue man, a product of a fusion of black, white, and Indian people.

Interracial marriages among Harlemites produced plenty of "hot copy" for the media, but they also provided models of talented Americans who refused to bow to the racial purists. Soon after she arrived in New York, Josephine Cogdell, the daughter of a wealthy Texas rancher, met the black Harlem intellectual George Schuyler, who wrote for the influential black newspaper the *Messenger*. A dancer and artist, Josephine married Schuyler in 1928, after a courtship carried out for several years in New York's night-club hot spots. For Josephine interracial love was not so new since she had seen her father and brother take black mistresses in Texas and "ridden after cattle with the colored cowboys, gone hunting and fishing with them and my nephews on moonlit nights and on rainy evenings played blackjack or poker with them on the back porch or in the big fragrant kitchens of one of our several homes." For Schuyler it was not so illogical either since one of his white great-grandfathers had fought in the Revolutionary War on the American side.

An heiress of the Cunard shipping line, Nancy Cunard, was another cultural rebel who found interracial love in Harlem. Marrying the black jazz pianist and singer Henry Crowder, she devoted herself to the causes of black Americans. Her scorching dissection of the trumped-up charges against the Scottsboro Boys, who were sent to prison on the perjured evidence of two white prostitutes who accused nine black youngsters of rape, was one of the many instances of her devotion to black America.

More numerous and lasting than New York interracial marriages were New York interracial intellectual and cultural ties. Through the twenties and thirties, Harlem was aboil with events and parties where whites and blacks met to discuss poetry, listen to music, watch dance performances, organize politically, or simply socialize. One such black-white intellectual tie linked Zora Neale Hurston to Franz Boas. Raised in a rural black township in north Florida, Hurston arrived in New York in 1925 and quickly fell in with such bright young talents as Langston Hughes. While studying at Barnard College, Hurston impressed Boas. This led to Hurston's gathering of black folktales from her native South and the publication of *Mules and Men* in 1935, the first collection of African-American folklore compiled by an African-American. Hurston maintained her intellectual ties with Boas for years as she resurrected, in passionate and moving stories, the folklore of rural southern blacks.

Drawn to the Harlem Renaissance, a number of blacks and whites became historians, archaeologists, and novelists of the African-American experience, promoting its importance and laying the groundwork for the rise of African-American history and black literature to come in the 1960s. For black Americans, the artists of the Harlem Renaissance created a body of art, music, and literature in which they "could see their own faces and features accurately and lovingly reflected." Among white Americans, the Renaissance fired the imaginations of those who still dreamed of America as a place of interconnected, if not fused, destinies.

Harlem was a political as well as cultural site of interracialism. The American Communist Party, which had paid little attention to black Americans until the 1930s, began to make inroads with black Americans in Chicago and Harlem in 1931, when it took up the cause of the Scottsboro Boys. Over the next few years the Communist Party attracted many of Harlem's cultural leaders, including Paul Robeson, who by the late thirties was a world-renowned actor and singer. The Communist Party was, at that time, the only political organization dedicated to breaking down the walls of racial bigotry and separation.

DEPRESSION AND WAR

The Great Depression took the steam out of the Harlem Renaissance. And the nation's most devastating economic collapse seems an unlikely place to look for a move against racism. After all, the intense competition for jobs at the bottom of the ladder might easily have intensified racial conflict. But so many Americans suffered through a decade of massive unemployment that the opposite seems to have occurred—a decline in lynching and urban race riots amid a creeping recognition among whites that their "natural advantages" did them little good in a time of crisis.

In the mid-1930s, the Congress of Industrial Organizations, led by a new militant group of labor leaders determined to organize workers on an industry-wide basis, took the first step to end the inflamed race relations that had kept white and black workers divided. Beginning with the steel industry, the CIO committed itself to interracial labor organizing. Moving from the steelworkers to the United Auto Workers, the National Maritime Union, and the Packinghouse Workers, the CIO began to bridge one of the biggest racial chasms in American society—in the workplaces where people earned their living. A black packinghouse worker in Chicago applauded the integration of the meatcutters: "I don't care if the union don't do another lick of work raising our pay, or settling grievances about anything. I'll always believe they done the greatest thing in the world getting everybody who works in the yards together, and breaking up the hate and bad feelings that used to be held against the Negro. We all doing our work now. . . . President of the local, he's Negro. First vice president, he's Polish. Second vice president, he's Irish. Other officers: Scotchman, Lithuanian, Negro, German." Bringing people of different ethnic ancestries together in workplaces was one of the vital steps toward imagining a mixed-race America.

Another partial solvent of racial hostility was the leadership of Eleanor Roosevelt. Much more than her husband, President Franklin D. Roosevelt, she crisscrossed the country, speaking on behalf of the cruel plight of African-Americans and condemning race discrimination. Even when her husband declined to endorse a federal antilynching law, Eleanor continued to speak out in favor of it. While he was worrying about losing the southern white vote in the 1944 presidential election, she was going to black colleges, housing projects, and homes, including a trip to Tuskegee Institute in Alabama, where she addressed 5,000 blacks in the campus chapel. Likewise, she urged FDR to use his executive powers to end the exclusion of African-Americans and Asian-Americans from the Army Air Corps, from all but mess and laundry positions in the Navy, even from the Army Dental

The black and white farmworkers pictured here were attending a meeting of the Southern Tenant Farmers' Union (STFU), organized in Arkansas in 1934. The STFU received national publicity for promoting interracial worker cooperation and nonviolence. It also came under attack because it was aligned with the American Socialist Party. Ironically, interracialism became identified in the white public's mind with alien influences. [University of North Carolina, Chapel Hill.]

Corps. The United States would fight the entire war with segregated units, but through Eleanor's persistence, FDR made some changes. One was to appoint Colonel Benjamin O. Davis, grandson of a slave, to the rank of brigadier general. This brought plenty of hate mail to the White House, such as a letter from an Illinois couple that said, "It is incomprehensible to normal Americans for you to appoint a member of the red, yellow, or black race to the high rank of Brigadier General." Still, the war brought a great many Americans of different skin shades into close contact, and thousands learned in combat zones that the race propaganda about black inferiority and mulatto degeneracy that they had heard before the war was untrue.

Black leaders, determined that the nation's shabby treatment of African-Americans would not continue while blacks gave their lives for the nation's defense, pushed to end discrimination in the booming defense industry. All over the country in 1941, blacks were frozen out of all but janitorial jobs. "We have not had a Negro working in 25 years and do not plan to start now," wrote Standard Steel in Kansas City. In California, Vultee Air announced: "It is not the policy of this company to employ other than of the Caucasian race." Threatened with a massive African-American march on Washington, and pushed hard by his wife, FDR yielded in June 1941 and issued Executive Order 8802, which called on employers and labor unions to end discrimination "because of race, creed, color or national origin." It also set up the Fair Employment Practices Commission (FEPC) to monitor compliance.

As a result of this executive order, millions of workers on the home front toiled alongside people of different races for the first time in their lives. This did not happen without strife or white hostility. Sneering at FDR's FEPC, the *Alabama Times* announced: "A bunch of snoopers, two of whom are Negroes, will assemble in Birmingham to determine whether the South is doing right by Little Sambo." But waves of women war workers began to find that color was only skin deep. One white Texas woman who worked alongside black women in a war factory recounted: "At first I thought I just couldn't do it. . . . I always thought colored people were not clean and smelled bad and weren't as good as white people. But these I have worked with at the plant are just as good as anybody." Another white worker recalled telling her supervisor in amazement: "I said good night to Mary tonight when she left. I actually told a colored girl good night." From such individual changes of heart, multiplied thousands of times as work sites became racially mixed during the war, came the dawning of a new era.

FRANCES FITZPATRICK OSATO:
REFUGEE FROM DEBUTANTISM

When the noted architect from New York, F. W. Fitzpatrick, took his seventeen-year-old daughter with him to Omaha, Nebraska, in 1914, he could hardly imagine the change in direction his daughter's life would take as a result. While her father worked on building Omaha's first skyscraper, Frances Fitzpatrick developed an interest in Japanese art. Soon the society-page editor of an Omaha newspaper wanted to write about her, and when he sent a photographer to shoot her picture, a romantic interest developed between Frances and the man behind the camera— Shoji Osato. The romance bloomed. But Frances knew that the course she was taking was perilous. Could she marry Shoji only a few years after Congress had passed the bill banning Japanese immigration and when many states had prohibited Asian-Caucasian marriage?

Frances Fitzpatrick returned to New York for a year to think about it and "test out her love." She soon realized that "she was bored to death" with the narrowness of her social position and was deeply interested in Japanese art. She was in love with Shoji. Her parents were "reluctant to see her marry" a Japanese man, she said. "I was the baby of the family and they thought that I was in too much of a hurry."

Nonetheless, Shoji Osato and Frances Fitzpatrick were married in 1916. "Mutual interest in Oriental art brought my husband and myself together," she later told a San Francisco newspaper as she was about to sail from San Francisco to Tokyo in 1923. "I gradually fell in love with him, and we were married when I was nineteen." The marriage took place in Iowa because justices of the peace in Nebraska refused to issue a marriage license. In 1923, by which time the marriage had produced two daughters, Frances Osato decided to take her children to Japan "to give them the benefit," as the newspaper expressed it, "of Nipponese cul-

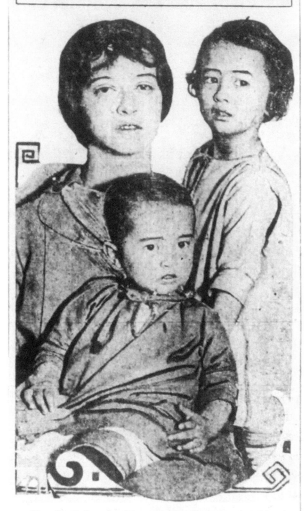

DOESN'T WANT FLAPPERS

Mrs. Shoji Osato, white wife of a Japanese, is taking her children to Japan to give them the benefit of Nipponese culture. She is shown here with her girls, Sona (right) and Teru.

In 1907, Congress passed a law that any woman (such as Frances Fitzpatrick Osato, pictured here) who married an "alien" automatically lost her citizenship. Congress designed this law to regulate the emotions of white American women and hence to prevent interracial children. When Frances Osato left for Japan with her two daughters in 1923, she left behind a nation that had deprived her of the vote guaranteed to women only three years before by passage of the Nineteenth Amendment. [*San Francisco Examiner.*]

ture." "My marriage to an Oriental has not made a gulf between me and my people," she explained to the reporter, "but there is a demureness and modesty about the Japanese that is prevalent in no other race. I want my little girls reared in such an environment."

The children of this marriage, Teru and Sona Osato, were described as "pretty little Eurasians" in the San Francisco press report at the time of their departure from the United States. Her little girls, Frances Osato told the press, "are the favorites of the fourteen grandchildren in the Fitzpatrick family." But they were soon to meet their other grandparents in Japan when their father opened a studio in partnership with Toyo Mukai, a famous Japanese artist.

Frances Fitzpatrick Osato was one of several hundred prominent Americans who defied social conventions by crossing racial boundaries in her time. Like many such renegades, she found across the racial boundary not only love but a culture in which she wanted her children to grow up. For the San Francisco newspaper reporter in 1923, Frances Osato was taking her daughters to "the land of cherry blossoms and chrysanthemums." But the reporter may have come closer to Frances Osato's motives when she told the readers of the *San Francisco Examiner* that "Teru and Sona Osato will not grow up to be American flappers, to call their father 'old dear' and pursue their young way in defiance of all authority, as American flappers are credited with doing."

RECAPTURING THE DREAM

Four years after the end of World War II, America's masters of the musical stage—Richard Rodgers and Oscar Hammerstein—did the forbidden. By gently weaving the nation's biggest social problem into a new musical in 1949, they violated the unspoken rule that politics and the musical stage don't mix. But *South Pacific* was a box-office bonanza. Drawing on James Michener's book *Tales of the South Pacific,* Rodgers and Hammerstein gave the public a musical story about love, boundary crossing, and pain. One cultural wall breacher was a middle-aged Frenchman who had fled Paris before World War II and found love in French Polynesia. From this tropical romance came two mixed-race children. When the U.S. Navy arrived, the now widowed French planter fell in love with Nellie Forbush, a nurse from Little Rock, Arkansas. Nellie's love for the Frenchman hit the rocks when she found herself unable to accept his earlier cross-race marriage. The other plot involves Joe Cable, a clean-cut Princeton-educated WASP who, as a naval officer, was fighting the Japanese in the Pacific. Far from home, the war-weary Cable falls in love with Liat, the beautiful, latte-colored sixteen-year-old daughter of Bloody Mary, a betel nut–chewing Polynesian woman who knows all about love that has no color distinctions. Aware that he cannot violate his nation's most enduring taboo by taking Liat back to Philadelphia, his hometown, Joe sings ruefully about the superficiality of racial barriers in what would become the show's most memorable song: "You've Got to Be Carefully Taught."

> You've got to be taught to hate and fear.
> You've got to be taught from year to year.
> It's got to be drummed in your dear little ear.
> You've got to be carefully taught.
>
> You've got to be taught to be afraid
> Of people whose eyes are oddly made
> And people whose skin is a different shade.
> You've got to be carefully taught.
>
> You've got to be taught before it's too late,
> Before you are six or seven or eight,
> To hate all the people your relatives hate.
> You've got to be carefully taught.

Rodgers and Hammerstein were pressured to eliminate the song because it would offend American racial sensibilities, but they stood their ground. Two legislators in Georgia vehemently protested. And in many southern cities opposition rose against even presenting the musical, but too many wanted to see this heart-tugging show about war, love, and discrimination for it to be silenced or censored. From its opening night in New York City on April 7, 1949, *South Pacific* was a thundering success. It played continuously to full houses for five years in New York, then opened in London, where it continued for two years, moved on to the Continent, made its way around the United States, and later was made into a movie. Three and a half million Americans saw it on stage in New York, millions more watched the movie, and countless millions listened to the phonograph record taken from it.

We can never really know exactly how Rodgers and Hammerstein's plea for racial tolerance affected popular attitudes about race mixing. But *South*

Pacific probably did more than all the social-science debunkers of scientific racism to move Americans away from notions of how "blood" determined character and race mixing threatened the nation. And white Americans who were thrilled by *South Pacific* had other, more concrete, reasons for trying to put racism behind them.

THE LESSONS WAR TAUGHT AMERICANS

By the time a million minority servicemen returned home from World War II, nearly a century had passed since Lincoln's Emancipation Proclamation. Black Americans, Mexican-Americans, American Indians, and Japanese-Americans, who had demonstrated their courage on the battlefield, were determined that the return of peace would not bring another era of rampant discrimination and exploitation. One sign of increasing black restive-

The members of A Battery, 349th Field Artillery Regiment, shown here at Fort Sill, Oklahoma, in about 1943, were part of a segregated army. Eleanor Roosevelt's efforts to enlist her husband in the campaign to integrate America's armed forces failed because FDR was afraid of losing the southern vote, which was thoroughly Democratic in this era. [Library of Congress.]

ness was the remarkable growth of the National Association for the Advancement of Colored People (NAACP) during the war—from 50,000 to 450,000. One black corporal from Alabama who had fought in the Battle of the Bulge spoke for black Americans: "I spent four years in the Army to free a bunch of Dutchmen and Frenchmen, and I'm hanged if I'm going to let the Alabama version of the Germans kick me around when I get home. No sirreee-bob! I went into the Army a nigger; I'm comin' out a *man*."

Many white Americans finally agreed that a man was a man regardless of his skin color, for the war had pushed Americans to understand themselves anew. The totalitarianism and intolerance of Hitler's Germany had led to the horrendous, genocidal Holocaust. The Nazi concentration camps vividly showed Americans how prejudice and propaganda about racial purity could turn even the most civilized and democratic society into a slaughterhouse. Hitler had done exactly what Madison Grant had suggested: a eugenics program to sterilize "defectives," followed by the extermination of "inferior" peoples. After Americans learned the full story of Hitler's "final solution" of the "Jewish problem," many found racialist talk vile. Within a single generation, calls for racial elimination went from being normal and popular to being the sign of extremism, even insanity.

In effect, Hitler had exposed the worst side of American racists and religious bigots. He did not, however, cleanse America of its most odious tendencies. Instead of asserting anti-Semitism publicly, people could retreat to a "gentleman's agreement"—the title of a much-read novel and much-watched movie after the war. But Hitler's Nazi Germany made it much harder to defend any racial or religious boundary in postwar United States. Frank Sinatra took the position "All races and religions, that's America to me" in the song "The House I Live In" (1946). A few years later, President Eisenhower told the nation that "Every American should have a religion and I don't care what it is." Intermarriage between Protestants and Catholics, Jews and Protestants, Catholics and Jews soon grew so rapidly that Jewish leaders began to fear that American Jewry would disappear.

By the end of the 1940s, it was no longer possible to sustain the naïve belief that African- or Hispanic- or Indian- or Asian-Americans were an inferior, innately doomed branch of humankind. Nor could American boasts about the virtues of democracy command respect abroad. The United States and the Soviet Union were in competition for the allegiance of dozens of Third World nations achieving postwar independence from their European colonial masters. Soviet spokesmen skillfully argued to the leaders of emerging nations in Africa, Asia, the West Indies, and the Middle East that socialism was color-blind while American democracy was a sham. And they had plenty of people of color who could testify to this. Foreign service officers repeatedly faced the troubling question about how America could be the "leader of the free world" when millions of its citizens were not free at all. "The race question," said the U.S. ambassador to Turkey in 1950, "is the sixty-four-thousand-dollar question fired at me wherever I go."

From the determination of America's religious and racial minorities and the realities of Cold War competition with the Soviet Union emerged the Civil Rights Movement. Actually, it had begun even before World War II was over. In 1944, when 10,000 white mass-transit workers in Philadelphia struck to protest the promotion of eight black employees to motormen, President Roosevelt broke the strike by ordering the Secretary of War to use the army to operate the subways and trolleys. Later that year, Roosevelt admitted the first black journalist to a presidential press conference, and the Supreme Court outlawed the "white primary," by which southern states excluded blacks from Democratic primary races (which in effect determined congressional victories, since the Republican Party was very weak in the South at this time). In 1946, President Truman appointed a Civil Rights Commission, whose report called for overturning segregation practices in every area of American society. In 1947, Jackie Robinson broke the color line in professional baseball, blazing the trail for athletes in other sports. In the same year, black reporters gained access to the Senate press gallery. In 1948, Truman sent the first presidential civil rights program to Congress since Reconstruction. Though southern Democrats made mincemeat of this bold program, the president—pushed hard by the black labor leader A. Philip Randolph—issued an executive order desegregating the armed forces. In the same year, the Supreme Court ruled that restrictive housing covenants, by which some white homeowners pledged not to lease or sell property to any non-Caucasian, were unconstitutional. Such covenants had made huge parts of American cities off-limits for people of color—in Chicago, 11 square miles; in St. Louis, 5.5 square miles; and likewise in almost every other American city.

All of these steps, like creeks merging to form a stream, and streams converging to create a river, heightened the general awareness that democracy could not coexist with racism and religious bigotry and that people of color were not the "Sambos" or "beasts" that had been portrayed in science, literature, politics, art, and music. None of this, however, meant that people would necessarily look across the color line to find mates. But when they met in desegregated public places, when they toiled at integrated workplaces, when they worshiped in mixed-race congregations, when they lived in multicultural neighborhoods, old stereotypes began to decay if not crumble. Interracial romance had a way of happening.

THE LAW STEPS IN

What took place in California after the war ended predicted the future of America. Thousands of servicemen returned home from the Pacific, and many came with wives who had never seen the United States. Congress almost *had* to act in 1947 to admit the Japanese and Chinese women whom American servicemen were marrying in surprising numbers after the war. The restrictive immigration act of 1924 banned virtually all Asian immigrants, but when German and Italian women were allowed to accompany GI husbands home after 1945, it became logically impossible to deny entry to American wives from Japan and China. No less a person than the commanding officer of the fabled "Flying Tigers," Major General Claire Chennault, had married a Chinese woman just after the war. Could a war hero not come home with his legal wife, Anna Chan Chennault?

Most Japanese and Chinese parents were appalled to see their daughters marry American soldiers and sailors, but love leaped over all obstacles erected both in Asian countries and the United States. In the twenty years after World War II, about 40,000 Japanese women followed their husbands to the United States. After the Korean War ended in 1955, thousands of Korean war brides made the same choice and were admitted on the same terms. The children of these marriages became thoroughly Americanized, though some mothers taught their children to take pride in their Japanese or Korean heritage. The children of black fathers and East Asian mothers generally regarded themselves as black Americans, though some found themselves rejected at black student unions or harassed by black women for dating black men. Some refused to identify themselves as black, insisting that they were bicultural and proud of both parts of their cultural inheritance. One daughter of a black father and Japanese mother insisted: "What I am is 'whole' Japanese and 'whole' American." The children of white fathers and Japanese mothers were usually accepted as Caucasians because their skin color was very light, and they were admired for their somewhat "exotic" features.

When Japanese war brides began arriving on the West Coast after World War II, the nation found itself facing a logical absurdity: an American serviceman could marry a Japanese woman overseas and bring her to his country as a marriage partner, but his brother who had served overseas could not return to California and marry a Japanese-American woman who had been born in his own town, had gone to school with him, and was thoroughly American in language and cultural habits.

This was the situation in 1948 when the California Supreme Court considered an appeal from Andrea Perez and Sylvester Davis, a young Los Angeles couple who challenged the law that prohibited interracial marriage. Perez was white and Davis was black. They knew that the Catholic church where they worshiped had no official objections to intermarriage. Yet a Los Angeles County clerk would not issue them a marriage license. Their lawyer argued that California's miscegenation law was an arbitrary and offensive restraint on their freedom of religion. In a four-to-three decision, the State Supreme Court agreed that the law was unconstitutional. Like the breaking of a logjam, this first state revocation of prohibitions on interracial marriage was followed quickly in other western and midwestern states.

FORBIDDEN LOVE

In the late 1940s many Chinese war brides attended English classes, such as this one in Minneapolis. Congress passed the War Brides Act in 1945, which allowed American servicemen to bring Chinese wives to America. Many of the husbands were Chinese-American themselves. The American occupation of Japan after 1945 resulted in thousands of Japanese brides coming "stateside" with their white American husbands. [Courtesy of Judy Yung.]

When the California Supreme Court overturned the law prohibiting interracial marriage, love began to transcend racial boundaries in a way that made earlier racial stereotypes seem ludicrous. The rise of marriages between white Americans and Asian-Americans was astonishing. Within a single generation, about half of the children of Japanese-American parents were choosing marital partners (mostly white) whom they would not have been allowed to marry legally at the end of World War II. This is compelling evidence of how fast attitudes could change. The sons and daughters of Japanese-Americans who had spent most of World War II in internment camps because white America regarded them with suspicion were taking into their homes the sons and daughters of those who had interned them.

Chinese-, Korean-, and Filipino-Americans were marrying across racial

Lena Horne and Lennie Hayton, after marrying in France in 1947, returned to New York on the *America*, where black stewards and stewardesses complained they could not join the maritime union. Hearing this, Lena refused to entertain first-class passengers at a shipboard benefit for the white crew's welfare fund. Her daughter, Gail Horne, married Sidney Lumet, a white Hollywood movie and television director, the day after the assassination of President Kennedy. [AP/Wide World Photos.]

lines at rates nearly as high as those of Japanese-Americans. At first, Asian-American parents were usually as opposed as white American parents to interracial marriages in their family. In the early 1950s, it was not uncommon for a Japanese-American or Chinese-American daughter marrying an "outsider" to be disowned by her parents, who believed she was abandoning an ancient and venerable culture. But these parents changed, as did white parents. Mixed-race grandchildren had a way of melting even the hardest hearts. Said one Japanese-American father: "I would prefer that [my children] marry a Japanese person but I feel that if the person they choose to marry is a nice person and I feel they are going to be happy, I'll be happy for them too." His wife agreed. "I'm leaving it up to the kids. . . . I would like to see that they marry *nihonjins* [one of ours] but it doesn't have to be."

Interracial couples in this brave new era faced both muttered slurs and open ostracism for following their hearts rather than bowing to deeply embedded customs. More than eyebrows were raised in 1947 when Lena Horne, Hollywood's most glamorous black female star, married Lennie Hayton, the son of Russian immigrants. Horne's career, since she'd danced in the chorus line at Harlem's Cotton Club in the 1930s at age sixteen, had taken off during World War II. In 1941, she became the first black performer signed by a major studio, and by war's end she was one of the black servicemen's favorite pinups. That the sultry Horne should marry a white piano-singer who played with Paul Whiteman's jazz and swing orchestra was shocking to black as well as white Americans.

Two years later, in 1949, Walter White, then the NAACP's executive director, divorced his African-American wife and married a white journalist and businesswoman named Poppy Cannon. This again caused a great stir. White had grown up in Atlanta and was an African-American by choice. Blond and blue-eyed, his skin was so light that he could easily have passed as white. Poppy Cannon's hair and skin were darker than White's. But White had learned early, when he stood with his father, rifle in hand, in front of their house to face down a white mob in search of black blood. He later wrote: "I knew then who I was. I was a Negro, a human being with an invisible pigmentation which marked me a person to be hunted, hanged, abused, discriminated against, kept in poverty and ignorance, in order that those whose skin was white would have readily at hand a proof of their superiority. . . ."

When White and Cannon married, they were attacked by white and black Americans alike. The black press indicted White for selling out his race for a white woman and vilified Cannon for seducing one of America's most eminent black leaders. White segregationists crowed that White was evidence of what they had argued for generations: that what black civil rights activists really wanted was possession of white women. In 1951, no

One of Walter White's greatest achievements was in leading the NAACP's campaign against segregation in the armed services. First raising this issue in 1940, he struggled for a decade until President Truman desegregated the military in 1950. He's pictured here in New Delhi with Poppy Ruskin Cannon, his wife. [AP/Wide World Photos.]

bank in New York City would give White and Cannon a loan to buy a house.

Die-hard racial purists, who in the 1950s still represented the majority position in America, liked to believe that those who intermarried were bohemian cultural rebels in Hollywood and New York or tasteless riffraff from society's lower class. But many intermarriages challenged such attitudes in the 1950s and 1960s. When the steel heiress Ann Mather, a blond Smith College graduate from Boston's tony Beacon Hill and a descendant of famous Puritan ministers, walked down the aisle in 1951 to marry Frank Montero, an African-American and an executive of the Urban League, plenty of jaws dropped, as the nation's best and brightest were seen putting old racial shibboleths behind them. The hostility to such life choices softened when in 1957 the wildly popular calypso singer and dancer Harry Belafonte married the stunning Julie Robinson, a Jewish dancer who for years had been the only white dancer in the Katherine Dunham troupe. The tabloid press speculated that this would ruin the performer's status on both sides of the color line. But white American women came to see him as a model partner, and black Americans admired the battles that Belafonte and his new wife waged against segregation and racism. No child of theirs could be labeled "degenerate" or "mongrel."

Other interracial celebrity marriages followed. Sammy Davis, Jr., went to the altar with the Swedish beauty May Britt in 1960. In the same year Eartha Kitt married a white California businessman, Bill McDonald. Charlayne Hunter-Gault, one of today's premier broadcast journalists, married Walter L. Stovall across the color line in 1963. Rock-and-roll star Chubby Checker married the winsome Dutch woman Catherina Lodders in 1964. Poet and novelist Maya Angelou took a white husband; and the basketball star Bill Russell and baseball hero Rod Carew married white women and raised interracial children. By the late 1960s, such marriages were hardly remarkable.

However, it was law, not love, that made the biggest change in the country. In 1965, Congress passed a new immigration law that demolished the National Origins Act of 1924, which for forty years had nearly ended Japanese and Chinese immigration and sharply curtailed immigration from

Southern and Eastern Europe. By accepting immigrants impartially from all parts of the world, the new law brought to America millions of pilgrims who earlier had been described as degenerate and inferior: Asians, Mexicans, Africans, and Jews. By greatly expanding the annual quota, Congress created a virtual stampede of Asian and Latino immigrants. More than 11 million immigrants entered the United States between 1965 and 1995, and the great majority of them were from Asia, Mexico, Central America, and the Caribbean. For those who still believed in maintaining a "white man's country," the Immigration Act of 1965 was a disaster. But Republicans and Democrats alike supported it because the nation craved labor from overseas, just as it had throughout most of its history. The face of America had literally been changed.

Two years after the country's doors swung open, the Supreme Court agreed to review a case that would unintentionally affect the millions of incoming immigrants. In accepting the case of *Loving v. Virginia,* the court took on the most important miscegenation case ever decided. Mildred Delores Jeter and Richard Perry Loving grew up in the little town of Central Point, Virginia, and dated each other as teenagers. Deciding to marry in 1958, and knowing that this was illegal in Virginia because he was white and she was black, they exchanged vows in Washington, D.C. The nation's capital had never banned racial intermarriage. When they returned to Virginia, Jeter and Loving framed their marriage license and hung it proudly on their living room wall. Several weeks later, the county sheriff and two deputies stormed through an unlocked front door in the middle of the night. Invading their bedroom, the lawmen hauled them from bed and arrested them for violating Virginia's 1924 Act to Preserve Racial Integrity. Tried and convicted, the Lovings were sentenced to a year in jail. However, the judge was willing to suspend the sentence if they agreed to leave Virginia at once and never return for twenty-five years.

Five years later, in 1963, the Lovings decided to appeal the Virginia conviction. The judge who had sentenced them in 1958, now sitting on a higher court, refused to reconsider the decision and sounded as if he was still reading Madison Grant's *The Passing of the White Race.* "Almighty God created the races white, black, yellow, malay and red, and he placed them on separate continents," read the judge. "And but for the interference with his arrangement there would be no cause for such marriages. The fact that he separated the races shows that he did not intend for the races to mix."

The Lovings persisted. By 1967, they had exhausted petitions to the Supreme Court of Appeals in Virginia and a federal appeals court. But the court of last resort, the United States Supreme Court, agreed to hear their case. Supporting the Lovings were the NAACP, a coalition of Catholic bishops, and the Japanese American Citizens League (JACL). The Lovings rested their argument on the constitutional guarantees of equal protection under the law and the fundamental right to marry.

The Lovings won. Condemning Virginia's 1924 law as clearly "designed to maintain White Supremacy," the Supreme Court declared it unconstitutional. The court explained that it "cannot conceive of a valid legislative purpose . . . which makes the color of a person's skin the test of whether his conduct is a criminal offense" and charged that "distinctions between citizens solely because of their ancestry" are "odious to a free people whose institutions are founded upon the doctrine of equality."

As was the case in many Supreme Court decisions, *Loving v. Virginia* had a cascade effect. In the ten years after the *Loving* decision, most states repealed or changed all statutes that defined "race." They cleansed their law books of the racial terminology that had been carefully built up for decades. Nowhere in the United States, for the first time in 300 years, could a sheriff, county clerk, minister, or judge stand between any woman and any man who wished to spend their lives together as marriage partners. The world's oldest and most powerful democracy at last gave its people free choice in marriage—an option that had been recognized for centuries almost everywhere else in the world. America finally adopted the position staked out by William Lloyd Garrison in 1831:

> The pursuit of happiness is among the inalienable rights of man . . . and no legislative body has a right to deprive him of it. . . . A union of the sexes is a matter of choice. . . . To limit this choice to a particular family, neighborhood or people is to impoverish and circumscribe human hap-

piness. . . . These propositions we conceive to be reasonable, plain, unde-
niable, self-evident. . . . The standard of matrimony is erected by affection and purity, and does not depend upon the height, or bulk, or color,
or wealth, or poverty of individuals. Water will seek its level; nature will
have free course; and heart will answer to heart.

No headlong rush over the racial walls occurred as miscegenation laws
disappeared from the law books. But even the most formidable barrier—
social resistance to black-white unions—was surmounted by thousands of
couples. In Maryland, for example, 566 black-white marriages occurred in
the first nineteen months after the state repealed its anti-intermarriage law
in 1969. Slowly, Americans of all skin colors began to change their mind
about mongrelization and the passing of the great white race. The racial
walls had not vanished, but brick by brick they were coming down. And
even more change was in the offing.

PEGGY RUSK: DIPLOMAT'S DAUGHTER

Peggy Rusk and Guy Smith are shown here leaving their marriage ceremony at the Stanford University Chapel on September 21, 1967. It was also the year when African-Americans first became big-city mayors—Carl Stokes in Cleveland, Ohio, and Richard Hatcher in Gary, Indiana—and for the first time a black American, Thurgood Marshall, took a seat on the Supreme Court. [AP/Wide World Photos.]

When Peggy Rusk met Guy Smith at the Rock Creek Park riding stable in Washington, D.C., in 1963, it was almost love at first sight. For four years they remained steady sweethearts—but in secret. Four years older, Guy went to Georgetown University and graduated the same year that Peggy entered Stanford. While Guy was awaiting call to active duty in Vietnam as a second lieutenant in the Air Force Reserve, they decided to get married. In a brief ceremony at Stanford's chapel, before family members and close friends, the only daughter of Georgia-born Dean Rusk, the nation's secretary of state, exchanged vows with the son of one of Washington's best-known black families. The Secret Service and campus police who surrounded the chapel could not keep reporters and photographers away. This was news.

Ebony magazine reported that "a massive shock wave of comment reached into every city and hamlet in the United States and spread throughout the world." Reactions ranged from "diatribes of shocked and aggrieved white supremacists to ridicule and satire of black power-ites." The wife of President Lyndon Johnson hoped "everything will go well" for the young couple.

The newlyweds themselves didn't see their marriage as so remarkable. They loved riding horses. They loved the study of history—the college major for both of them. They came from families that were close-knit, devoted to their children, and, above all, determined to make the world a better place to live in. Guy Smith's mother, a Howard University graduate, was a schoolteacher for thirty-three years. His father, also a Howard graduate, was a social worker and social activist in the cause of racial equality. Peggy Rusk came from a family that was far more affluent and famous but much like her husband's family when it came to acting on what one believed in. As a young army intelligence officer in World War II, her father had listened to fellow officer Ralph Bunche's complaint that African-Americans were not permitted to eat in an officers' mess in the nation's capital. "We'll change that right now," said Rusk, and escorted Bunche to dinner. When Rusk became an international figure as secretary of state during the Vietnam War, he and his wife refused to join any country club that practiced racial discrimination, which meant nearly all the country clubs in the Washington area in the 1960s. Peggy's brother worked as associate director of the Urban League. As far as the young lovers were concerned, about the only thing they didn't have in common was the color of their skin.

THE END OF WALLS?

Filling out a form a few years ago for her three-year-old daughter's Social Security card, Laurie Gantt paused when she reached the box labeled "race." Laurie Gantt is white, her husband is black. But the "race" box asked whether the applicant was black or white. The toddler, of course, was both. So Laurie wrote "biracial." His brow furrowed, the white official in suburban Atlanta, Georgia, looked at the application and snapped, "What's this?" Gantt replied, "None of the categories apply. She's not any one of these. She's biracial." The bureaucrat looked at Laurie's three-year-old, scratched out the word "biracial," and put an X in the box marked "Black." "She's got to be one of them," he insisted and turned away to peer at another form.

Approaching the end of the century, many Americans are challenging officials of all kinds because they are fed up with the nation's mind-set about race. In forms that record their personal lives, they want their descent identified accurately, not by what Americans of previous generations thought about race. Some regard this attempt to put the nation's most enduring problem of race behind us as an intentional attack on the affirmative-action policies created to correct centuries of racial discrimination. But contention over how to count race may be only a bump in the path along which hundreds of thousands of Americans are moving—directly toward the altar where Americans of different racial ancestries are exchanging marriage vows as never before in our history. How and why this is happening is the focus of this chapter.

THE BOUNDARY-CROSSING REVOLUTION

Just as *South Pacific* began to soften the hostility of Americans toward people of different skin shades, movies began to change American attitudes in the 1960s and 1970s. From 1930 through the mid-1960s, Hollywood writers, directors, and producers had obeyed the Motion Picture Production Code that set interracial marriage off-limits, listing it alongside sexual perversion and venereal disease as improper subjects for American movies. Gingerly, filmmakers attempted to test the code in 1957 with *Island in the Sun,* in which Harry Belafonte played the role of a militant crusader for black rights who falls in love with a liberal white woman, played by the blond film star Joan Fontaine. The marriage never happens in the script. In 1965, Hollywood got bolder with *A Patch of Blue,* the touching story of a blind white girl (Elizabeth Hartman) who falls in love with an older black man (Sidney Poitier) who reciprocates her love and asks her to marry him. One blind, the other color-blind, the couple marries, in the face of a hostile society and an uncertain future. In the same year, Bernie Hamilton, a black actor, and Barbara Barrie, a white actress, fall in love on the silver screen in *One Potato, Two Potato.* They confront ugly harassment from both white and black Americans, but their love endures.

These films never reached masses of people, either because they went beyond mainstream tastes or lacked marquee star appeal. That changed in 1967 when Hollywood celebrities Spencer Tracy and Katharine Hepburn nudged millions of moviegoers to a new level of consciousness. In *Guess Who's Coming to Dinner,* Sidney Poitier, the rising black film star, made interracial love seem almost commonplace, while both sets of parents of the

After the Supreme Court ruled in 1954 that segregated public schools were unconstitutional, some filmmakers in Hollywood introduced more movies with racial themes. Sidney Poitier, pictured here in *A Patch of Blue*, was Hollywood's favorite black male star in the 1960s and 1970s. By contrast, Harry Belafonte got "doomed outlaw" roles. [*A Patch of Blue* © 1965 Turner Entertainment Co.]

young lovers just get used to it—though, ominously, the interracial newly-weds leave the country one day after the nuptials.

While it changed the attitudes of some, *Guess Who's Coming to Dinner* also *reflected* changing views. Hollywood would not have risked such a movie if the notion of interracial love hadn't already become acceptable among a sizable part of the population. Four years later, in 1971, a Harris poll proved this to be the case. It showed that one of every three Americans in their early twenties had dated across racial lines.

Momentum also grew out of racial chic in the Civil Rights Movement. Liberal white Americans, acting like some white abolitionists of the 1840s, cultivated friendships with black Americans and worked with them in the movement. This often led to interracial romance. Yet when it occurred between black male and white female activists, it often displeased both African-American women and white men working for civil rights.

While the Civil Rights Movement brought many people together in a quest for racial equality in America, interracial love went from forbidden to high-profile in the mass media. The ultimate seal of approval was conferred on interracial sex in 1985 when *Playboy* magazine, which catered principally to the sexual fantasies of white males, featured Grace Jones, a black actress, model, and cult figure, parading in the buff across six pages of the magazine with her Swedish boyfriend, Dolph Lundgren, the former European kick-boxing champion. Jones had already appeared in the James Bond movie *A View to a Kill*, where she made love with Agent 007.

In the nineties, moviegoers and television watchers regularly see interracial romance and marriage. In *The Joy Luck Club*, *White Men Can't Jump*, *The Rich Man's Wife*, *The Bodyguard*, and *Waiting to Exhale*, partners from different racial backgrounds find color no obstacle to love. Television programs with interracial dating and marriage faze only the hard-core defenders of America's racial boundaries.

In the 1970s and 1980s, the trickle of people marrying across racial boundaries became a stream, as Americans learned literally to love thy neighbor. In 1960, about 150,000 new American marriages were interracial, most of them involving white partners marrying Asian-American or Hispanic-American spouses—a huge increase from a generation before when most states prohibited interracial marriage. Since then, the rate of interracial marriage has doubled every decade, from 310,000 marriages in 1970 to 1.2 million in 1992. The most frowned-upon kind of intermarriage, between black and white Americans, has grown apace. In 1970, the U.S. Census Bureau recorded 65,000 black-white marriages. A decade later, census takers found about 168,000 black-white marriages, and the number rose to more than 200,000 by 1988.

To be sure, this represented only a tiny fraction of all marriages in the United States, and was much lower than the rate of Japanese-American or Chinese-American outmarriage. Yet what had been nearly unthinkable a generation before was now regarded as acceptable by a majority of blacks and whites. By 1997, more than 60 percent of all white Americans and three-quarters of all black Americans approved of black-white marriage. Considering that all but 4 percent of white Americans opposed white black marriage in 1958 and that in 1972 three-quarters of whites and 40 percent of blacks were still opposed, this was a huge shift in public opinion within a single generation. Almost lost from memory were the statements of the nation's most respected scientists of a century before claiming that white-black intercourse was "a sin against nature, as incest in a civilized community is a sin against purity of character," and that "hybridism is heinous" and "mulattoes are monsters." How slack jawed these scientists would be today to hear Art Westinen, a thoroughly suburban white father, maintain, "It's neat to be able to say I'm part black." A recent DNA test proved conclusively that the Westinens of Staten Island are directly descended from Eston Hemings, the youngest son Sally Hemings had during her thirty eight-year sexual relationship with Thomas Jefferson.

The trendsetters in interracial marriage, as in so many other aspects of cultural change, are the young. In some parts of the country, such as Los Angeles County, about 20 percent of the Generation Xers who have married recently have tied the knot with a partner of a different race. Almost one of every five African-American males in their twenties has a non-black spouse. The rate is even higher among young Latino males who have gone to the altar.

When American advertising, the mighty engine of American consumerism, finally got on the interracial bandwagon, it was clear that an age-old taboo was in tatters. By the late 1980s, international clothes merchandisers realized that interracial love was a phenomenon that could be used to sell their products. Calvin Klein ads featured a bare-chested young white man embracing a dark-skinned, nappy-haired woman. Ads for Guess jeans showed a handsome black man with his hands around the waist of a very blond, young white woman. This was not an attempt to change the way Americans saw themselves or to pave the way toward smoother race relations. Powerful corporate managers in charge of advertising campaigns— Calvin Klein and Guess executives among them—live and die by the bottom line, the profits announced at the annual shareholders conference. If the voters of Tuskegee, Alabama, could elect a black man, Johnny Ford, as their mayor in 1978 when he was married to a white woman, and if conservative Republicans, once fiercely opposed to interracial marriage, could elect Phil Gramm to the Senate in 1984 with a Japanese-American wife at his side, then featuring interracial love in ad campaigns aimed at young shoppers made good financial sense.

ENGINES OF CHANGE

Why did so many people, within a few decades, trample racial boundaries that had been so carefully policed and emotionally defended for so many generations? And why did the disgust with previous definitions of race begin to accelerate during the Civil Rights Movement when black pride, red pride, and brown pride seemed to argue against interracial liaisons and multiracial identity?

One key force for change was global migration of a kind that the nation had never before seen. In the last three decades, millions of immigrants from Mexico, Asia, Central America, and the Middle East have added to the American mosaic. The countries of origin were those that white Protestant America had traditionally shunned. In 1940, about half a million Asian-Americans lived in the United States. That number grew to 5 million by 1985 and 10 million by 1997. The Latino percentage of the American population grew from less than 5 percent to 11 percent between 1960 and 1997. It is projected that by the end of this century, only one in six Americans will be able to trace direct descent from white Europeans. Always multicultural, America is moving toward a time when "whites" will be a minority.

Such gigantic demographic shifts have made it nearly impossible to maintain a concept of Americanness built on the white race and on white racial purity. After thirty years of streaming into southern California, Central American and Mexican immigrants have made everyone see their past in a new way. The Anglo population that had numerically dominated Los Angeles for many decades regarded the ubiquitous Spanish place names— the Santa Monica and San Gabriel mountains, the towns of San Pedro, El Monte, and Loma Linda, the missions at San Juan Capistrano, La Purisma Concepcion, and Monterey—as little more than quaint reminders of a romantic Spanish past. But now the shifting ethnic mix has driven home the point that if southern California has become markedly multicultural, it had also been so generations ago. California was not simply the destination of millions of new immigrants; rather it was being re-Hispanicized. It is almost as valuable to know Spanish in the American Southwest at the end of the twentieth century as it had been in the eighteenth.

In Hawaii the warm weather playground of so many American and Japanese vacationers—interracial marriage is now the norm rather than the exception, and this has obliged visitors to rethink the nation's past. The westernmost frontier of the United States—and its fiftieth state—has long been a mid-ocean site of racial interchange. Chinese, Russians, Aleuts, Fijians, African-Americans, and Europeans were mingling their blood there by the 1840s. When sugar became the Hawaiian Islands' cash crop, contract labor agents brought men in from every point of the compass. The largest number came from China, Korea, Japan, Portugal, Puerto Rico, and the Philippines. But smaller numbers arrived also from Norway, Germany, Spain, Russia, Mexico, and Samoa. Arriving overwhelmingly as unmarried young men, they mixed extensively with Hawaiian women. Now, many decades later, mixed-race people predominate in Hawaii. Except for new immigrants to the state, people of unmixed racial backgrounds will soon be a rarity. This has put pressure on every definition of American society that stresses its white cultural heritage. One Hawaiian woman whose ancestry is Hawaiian, Caucasian, and Chinese and who is married to a Caucasian says, "I don't know . . . what 'Hawaiian' is—I feel it is the place, not the *race*."

While population shifts undermined notions of racial purity, the integration of schools, workplaces, and public spaces encouraged people to leap over previously guarded racial walls in choosing friends or life partners. Especially when integration brought people together on roughly equal terms, the chances for interracial friendship or romance jumped. The armed forces became gigantic employers of integrated personnel and powerful promoters of interracial cooperation. The greater the equality, in such situations as liv-

In this tourist promotion picture celebrating Hawaii's exotic ambience, the women on the top row, left to right, are Chinese, Japanese-Portuguese, and Hawaiian-Dutch; on the bottom row, left to right, Portuguese, Chinese-Hawaiian-European, and Chinese-Hawaiian. [Courtesy, U.S. Information Agency.]

ing together in a college dorm or working together in an insurance office, the more likely it was that people of different skin hues and cultural ancestries would find attractive qualities in each other. By the 1970s, the invisible Berlin Wall of race was coming down, stone by stone. Human emotions—the attraction of individual Americans to each other regardless of race and religion and much else—ran ahead of group or national ideology.

When massive racial boundary crossing occurred, the natural, unstoppable result was a multiracial baby boom. Without doubt, this has caused some identity confusion and anguish, as it has in the past. If my mother is white and my father is black, what am I? If my father is white and my mother is Japanese-American, what is my racial identity? For many generations, the "one-drop" mentality obliged a child of a mixed marriage to identify with the parent of darker skin. This in effect disacknowledged the heritage of one parent. Even while attitudes were softening on strict racial categorization, the rise of racial pride and racial solidarity put an intense pressure on young Americans to make a single racial choice. For example, the son of an interracial marriage who went to a largely white university faced a difficult set of problems. To date a coed who was white like his mother could bring abuse from black female classmates and accusations of "betraying his race" and running after "white goddesses." To prefer not to live in an all-black dormitory invited scorn from members of the Black Student Union, who might scoff that he should be more like his father.

Many interracial couples have fought this tug-of-war. They had wanted their children to be proud of both parents and not to prefer grandparents, aunts, uncles, and cousins on one side of the family at the expense of the other side. They hoped that Americans would see some virtue in the fact that Booker T. Washington's father was white or that Martin Luther King, Jr., had an Irish grandmother and some American Indian ancestry as well.

Pride in racial mixing and pride in descent from different races led to the creation of multiracial social clubs in many cities where strength in numbers helped deal with these tensions. Manasseh clubs in Chicago and Milwaukee, named after the half-Egyptian son of the Old Testament's Joseph, sprang up in the 1890s and became prominent social organizations. One hundred couples, all of them with mixed-race children, founded New York

City's Penguin Club in 1936. In the 1940s, Los Angeles had its Club Miscegenation, where multiracial couples and their children could affirm their dual heritages. These were the pioneering clubs of the suppressed and scorned Americans who dared to oppose the color coding that entrapped white and black Americans alike.

Now in a period when greatly increased interracial marriage has produced a multiracial baby boom, racially mixed young Americans have formed dozens of organizations to help people cope with identity confusion and resist the pressure to identify with only one race. Berkeley, California, is home to an organization named Miscellaneous. Los Angeles has its Multiracial Americans of Southern California. Chicago has its Biracial Family Network. In Philadelphia, Atlanta, and Houston can be found branches of the Interracial Family Alliance. Omaha has its Parents of Interracial Children. On scores of college campuses, students form similar organizations in order to resist racial reductionism—the one-dimensional construction of their identity. Through strength in numbers, they demonstrate that identity has many layers, racial and otherwise. The first class on People of Mixed Race Descent taught at the University of California, Berkeley, in 1983 enrolled twenty-three students. In 1996, 226 students jostled for room in the lecture hall, and the waiting list grew. The course instructor, Terry Wilson, son of a Potawatomi father from an Oklahoma Indian reservation and a white mother, says: "Those of us of mixed racial descent embody the cutting edge of race relations. We're living reminders that the lines are there but the lines get crossed all the time."

THE PROBLEMS OF PROGRESS

No country can undergo massive shifts in attitudes and behavior without bitter disagreements, political maneuvering, and long periods of adjustment. If birthing is a painful process, so is rebirth. In overturning our racial code, notable disputes have emerged.

One vexing issue concerns how our government, at the local, state, and national levels, will deal with redefinitions of racial categories. The impatience of thousands of determined mixed-race Americans with fixed racial categories is forcing great bureaucracies to change. All over the country, parents and their children are insisting that college, government, and business officials abandon racial categories used on application forms and other documents that oblige them to answer questions that make them disavow part of their family. Twelve-year-old Kaleena Crafton, who lives in Redford, Michigan, wrote federal officials in 1995: "I find something wrong with how people define my racial category. To them, I'm either 'black,' 'white,' or 'Native American/Pacific Islander.' Well, I'm really European, African, and Native American. To me (and others), this is a problem. . . . When someone says I'm white or black, it is really lying about my heritage. Yes, lying. Because my race is not black, not white, and not Native American. It is multiracial. This category is important to me, so that I leave out none of my races." In 1995, at the University of California, Berkeley, a student whose four grandparents were Japanese, African-American, American Indian, and white was in danger of not receiving a diploma because she would not pick a conventional racial category on university forms. "I'm not going to deny three-quarters of my heritage to satisfy somebody else's ridiculous notions about race," she said.

Two lobbying groups, the Association of Multi-Ethnic Americans and Project RACE, have already pushed eight states—Maryland, Ohio, Illinois, Georgia, Michigan, Indiana, North Carolina, and Florida—to include a multiracial category on all school forms. Ramona E. Douglass, president of the Multi-Ethnic Americans in California, says, "Part of being a full American is saying who you are. I refuse to have someone pick for me."

Arguments over how to conduct the census in the year 2000 provide a vivid example of the ripsaw effect that new mixed-race affinities have produced. Organizations of Americans who are themselves biracial or whose children are biracial demand the end of Statistical Policy Directive No. 15, which since 1977 has laid down rules requiring all federal forms to specify the applicant's race as Alaskan/Native, Asian/Pacific Islander, Black, or White but also ask those filling out forms whether they are of "Hispanic origins" or not. These categories have been indispensable in monitoring compliance with civil rights laws, including the Voting Rights Act of 1965.

They are also used to determine whether police and firefighting forces are meeting court-ordered goals to diversify their workforces. All fifty states and thousands of municipalities use these racial categories to monitor public school enrollment, scholarship applications, and mortgage loans.

Yet after thirty years of affirmative action, public opinion has shifted so much that many politicians demand a rethinking of these policies, well intended though they were. Some argue that the problem can be solved by adding a mixed-race box for the census takers to check.

Others feel that a multiracial category may simply codify the difference between light- and dark-skinned African-Americans, as long as color remains a meaningful social marker in the minds of employers, landlords, and school admissions officers. Furthermore, many black leaders worry that black political and economic clout will shrink if large numbers of those who had previously identified themselves as African-American peel off, preferring to call themselves biracial or multiracial. They believe that "multiracial families pushing this movement are pawns for racists, whose real goal is to eliminate racial categories altogether, pushing the nation toward this delusion of a color-blind society." With all racial categories eliminated, government safeguards meant to promote equal opportunity for racial minorities would disappear. "To relinquish the notion of race—even though it's a cruel hoax—at this particular time," writes Jon Michael Spender, a professor of Afro-American Studies at the University of North Carolina, "is to relinquish our fortress against the powers and principalities that still try to undermine us."

When a Clinton Administration task force completed a long and exhaustive study of this question in July 1997, it took a middle-of-the-road position: although the study recommended that the Bureau of the Census should not add a "multiracial" category on the Census of 2000, still, recognizing the claims of mixed-race Americans, it suggested that citizens should be free to check off more than one racial category—as many as they wished. "I love the idea of having it be 'check as many as you identify with,' " said Cynthia Nakashima, instructor of a multiracial heritage course at UC Berkeley. "It says you don't have to be one or the other. It does more than a multiracial stand-alone box would have [done]."

This is a pragmatic solution to a problem that will not disappear anytime soon. Individual Americans can claim membership in as many racial groups as they chose. But by not adding a "multiracial" category, the Census Bureau ensured the continuance of two important steps that had been taken over several decades to redress the problems that race categorization had caused in the first place. First, any policy maker or social analyst can use data from the 2000 census to make comparisons with data from earlier censuses in order to chart the nation's progress in overcoming long-standing racial inequalities. Second, the compromise solution will retard the dilution of minority voting districts and prevent the reduction of government and private support for minority programs that are based on census figures. "The numbers drive the dollars," aptly noted Thomas C. Sawyer, chair of a House of Representatives committee that held hearings on changes for the 2000 census.

Even if the tide of American sentiment is shifting toward viewing skin color and "race" as irrelevant to the issue of love and marriage, tide pools of old-fashioned racism surely remain. In 1994, the tiny town of Wedowee, Alabama, populated by about 800 people, made national headlines when the high school principal called an assembly and asked the students if any of them intended to go to the senior prom with a date of a different race. Karen Parker, a sixteen-year-old, remembers that "a majority raised their hands," not really because they were dating across racial boundaries in the deep South but because "we just wanted to see what he was going to say." Principal Hulond Humphries declared that he would cancel the prom rather than allow any racially mixed couple to attend. ReVonda Bowen, whose father is white and mother is black, then stood up and asked the principal what race her date should be. He told her he could not think of an appropriate date for her because, as he put it, she was a biological "mistake" and it was his job to keep such mistakes from happening again. The young woman burst into tears. In the days that followed, all hell broke loose in Wedowee: the school board suspended the principal; a local Ku Klux Klan "Great Titan" declared that the principal was just "sticking up for the Bible"; 1,800 white citizens in the area signed a petition supporting Principal Humphries; and the mayor of this one-traffic-light town announced that

"We're way beyond" the race situation of twenty years ago when "an interracial couple walking down the street would make everybody stop, turn around, and look." Then, with tempers running high, the high school mysteriously burned to the ground. The combination of race and sex—a volatile mixture in the South for three centuries—proved to be still combustible. But a generational shift was clearly visible, with interracial teenage dating no longer rare in the heart of the old Confederacy, while older people, whatever their race, remained leery if not downright hostile to it.

America's resistance to its real mixed-race character has given way to an open and massive rush toward interracial relationships and marriages. Today, a wave of mixed-race children embrace the variety of their ancestors. This epic cultural shift promises the fulfillment of the old American quest for *e pluribus unum*—creating one out of the many, constructing commonalities out of diversity. Pocahontas, Wendell Phillips, Frederick Douglass, Lucy Parsons, Emma Ellen Howse Fong, José Vasconcelos, Lena Horne, and all the other racial wall breachers and racial cross-pollinators would welcome the late-twentieth-century scene. But they would probably also worry about the racial fissures that have accompanied racial fusion as the boundaries of race have crumbled.

As Americans argue over issues of multiculturalism (a slippery word in itself), about identity politics, about affirmative action, compensatory programs, and entitlements, they are entangled in an old tension between racial and religious essentialism on the one hand and racial and religious in-betweenness on the other that is worldwide in scope. In nearly every corner of the earth, those who celebrate boundary crossing and the melding of people of different ancestries are arguing fiercely with fundamentalists and essentialists who fear the dilution of their faith or "race." Events of recent years in Sarajevo, Sri Lanka, and Rwanda have shown that when rigid racial and religious categories are invoked, and ancient ethnic, racial, and religious hatreds are unleashed, horrendous brutality and genocidal "cleansing" can be the result.

In 1988, an immigrant from the old British Empire who had crossed many cultural boundaries himself wrote a novel that so offended religious essentialists that they put a million-dollar bounty on his head to snuff out his voice. The man was Salman Rushdie, and his enemies were Islamic fundamentalists who hated racial and religious mixing and feared it as surely as did the most rabid white Anglo-Saxon racial-purity writers of the early twentieth century. Writing in defense of his controversial novel, *The Satanic Verses*, Rushdie explained that those who hated him for writing about a group of British Muslims who were struggling with mixed identities "are of the opinion that intermingling with a different culture will inevitably weaken and ruin their own." Taking the opposite view, he spoke of how *The Satanic Verses* celebrated "hybridity, impurity, intermingling, the transformation that comes of new and unexpected combinations of human beings, cultures, ideas, politics, movies, songs. It rejoices," he continued, "in mongrelization and fears the absolutism of the Pure. Mèlange, hotchpotch, a bit of this and a bit of that is how newness enters the world. It is the great possibility that mass migration gives the world, and I have tried to embrace it." *The Satanic Verses,* he concluded, "is for change-by-fusion, change-by-conjoining. It is a lovesong to our mongrel selves."

Rushdie's words, as well as the price put on his head, remind us of the cost of clinging to racial absolutes. If we can learn from this, in tempering claims about racial essentialness, people abroad can learn from us. Those who have looked to America as a place of freedom and opportunity can see the rise of the *idea* of a mixed-race America where interraciality is becoming something to regard as a national strength. Few argue that universal intermarriage is needed to bring us together; nobody insists that we will reach the promised land only when all our grandchildren are shades of tan. But step by step, America and the world are learning that when people are allowed to make life partnership choices, when "heart answers to heart," the world's future is more secure because it is unshackled from the socially constructed category of race. The words "amalgamationism" and "mongrelization" have come a long way in the course of the twentieth century. Is the possibility of a mestizo America and a mestizo world at hand?

ELDRICK "TIGER" WOODS: MULTIRACIAL GOLFER

Tiger Woods, holding his trophy, poses with his mother, Kultida, in Bangkok after winning the Asian Honda Classic on February 9, 1997. [AP/World Wide Photos.]

When he joined the army, Earl Woods knew he was black—an African-American who had suffered his share of racial abuse. Growing up in America in the 1940s, it was only natural that he would marry a black woman. For many years of marriage, they never entertained the notion of any other racial classification than "black." That's how the army records had it, how his census entries had it, and how everyone around him had it—even though he knew that one of his grandparents was Native American and another was Chinese.

When Woods left for a second tour of duty in Vietnam, where he led a contingent of Green Berets, he arrived in the war-torn country as a divorced man. Then the U.S. Army sent Lieutenant Colonel Woods to Bangkok on assignment. Stationed there, he met and fell in love with Kultida, a pretty, young woman who identified herself as Thai, though in fact one of her grandparents was European and another was Chinese. In 1969, Kultida came back to the United States with Earl Woods and there they married.

Six years later, Kultida Woods gave birth to a boy. If all of the infant's eight great-grandparents had been there to welcome him home in his mother's arms from the hospital in Cypress, California, they would have been a pretty good representation of the state's increasingly diverse ethnic mix. Of the eight, one was Native American, two were African-American, two were European, two were Thai, and one was Chinese. What did that make Eldrick "Tiger" Woods?

Working out his own racial identity on his own terms, Tiger Woods has given a tremendous boost to the proud acknowledgment of mixed racial heritage. Growing up, he knew that his schoolmates regarded him as black—and sometimes taunted him for it. And as he became known as a golfing prodigy, breaking 80 on a regulation course by age eight and nailing holes-in-one by the time he was thirteen, he began to refuse identifying himself by only one part of his racial ancestry. By the time he won his record-setting third consecutive U.S. Amateur title at age twenty-one and a year later won the Masters Golf Tournament, beating his closest challenger by a record-setting twelve strokes, Woods began to teach sportswriters about more than golf.

Interviewing Tiger Woods, journalists were flummoxed. Bound by age-old racial categories—white, black, Indian, Asian—they didn't know what to make of Tiger's mixed ancestry. Eager to celebrate him as the first black golfing star, the equivalent of tennis's Arthur Ashe, they just wanted to call him African-American.

But Tiger wouldn't have it. At first he described himself as half-black and half-Thai. In 1996, when asked in Augusta, Georgia, how he felt about being the first black to win the Masters—a tournament that had banned all but white golfers until a few years ago—Tiger replied that he was proud to be the first black *and* the first Asian-American to win the fabled green blazer awarded to the Masters champ. Later he readily pointed out that in fact his family tree has more branches than two.

Tiger prevailed. In the sports columns today, he is one of America's greatest golfers. Leaving the old system of classifying people by race in tatters, he is now rarely identified by race. After all, how could a sportswriter submit a story about how Tiger Woods, "the phenomenal black-Chinese-Indian-Thai-European golfer," eagled the fourteenth hole with a staggering 346-foot drive, a 197-foot 7-iron shot that brought him to 8 feet from the cup, and a superbly confident putt?

Notes

(Numbers in **boldface** type indicate pages on which sources are cited.)

THE AMERICA THAT MIGHT HAVE BEEN

Students who have seen the Disney movie *Pocahontas* can test Hollywood's version of the American past by examining how two industrious historians have reconstructed the story of Pocahontas and John Rolfe's interracial marriage: Grace Steele Woodward, *Pocahontas* (Norman: University of Oklahoma Press, 1969), and Philip L. Barbour, *Pocahontas and Her World* (Boston: Houghton Mifflin, 1970). For John Smith's comment on Powhatan's people (**4**) see Edward Arber and A. G. Bradley, eds., *Travels and Works of Captain John Smith,* vol. I (Edinburgh: J. Grant, 1910), 8–9. For Rolfe's thoughts on his marriage to Pocahontas (**7**), see Barbour, *Pocahontas and Her World,* 247–52.

The invention of the word "miscegenation" (**8**) can be followed in David G. Corly, *Miscegenation: The Theory of the Blending of the Races, Applied to the American White Man and Negro* (New York: H. Dexter, Hamilton, 1864); a fascinating introduction to this pamphlet is Julius Marcus Bloch, *Miscegenation, Melaleukation, and Mr. Lincoln's Dog* (New York: Schaum, 1958).

How Indian-English relations unfolded in early Virginia is the subject of Karen Kupperman's *Settling with the Indians: The Meeting of English and Indian Cultures in America, 1580–1640* (Totowa, NJ: Rowman and Littlefield, 1980). The quotations from Robert Beverley and William Byrd (**8**) are taken respectively from Beverley, *The History and Present State of Virginia,* ed. Louis B. Wright (Chapel Hill: University of North Carolina Press, 1947), 159; and Byrd, *William Byrd's Histories of the Dividing Line Betwixt Virginia and North Carolina* (Raleigh: North Carolina Historical Commission, 1929), 3–4. For Thomas Jefferson's comments on intermixing with Native Americans (**9**), see Andrew A. Lipscomb, ed., *The Writings of Jefferson,* vol. X (Washington, DC: Thomas Jefferson Memorial Association, 1905), 363; and William B. Parker, ed., *Thomas Jefferson: Letters and Addresses* (New York: Sun Dial Classics, 1908), 190.

Houston's tumultuous life can be followed in the readable biography by Marshall De Bruhl, *Sword of San Jacinto: A Life of Sam Houston* (New York: Random House, 1993). Houston's comment about preferring Indian society (**9**) is taken from Charles Edwards Lester, *The Life of Sam Houston: The Hunter, Patriot, and Statesman of Texas* (Philadelphia: J. E. Potter, 1867), 22. Jackson's remark on Houston (**10**) can be found in De Bruhl, *Sword of San Jacinto,* 107. The quotations regarding Ooleteka's welcome to Houston, Houston's rights as a citizen of the Cherokee Nation, and his adoption of Cherokee ways (**10–11**) are drawn from Jack Gregory and Rennard Strickland, *Sam Houston and the Cherokees* (Austin: University of Texas Press, 1967), 9, 23, 29. For Houston's drinking problem and the quotation about it (**12**), see the peppy biography by Marquis James, *The Raven: A Biography of Sam Houston* (Indianapolis: Bobbs-Merrill Co., 1929), 157. Houston's remarks regarding the annexation of Texas (**14**) are given in De Bruhl, *Sword of San Jacinto,* 168–69.

For more about the "reality" of race (**17**), see Sidney Mintz, "Toward an Afro-American History," *Journal of World History* 13 (1971), 318. A good place to begin reading about race is Ashley Montagu, *The Concept of Race* (London: Collier-Macmillan, 1964). Also useful is an older work of one of the most important pioneers of interracial studies: Robert E. Park, *Race and Culture* (Glencoe, IL: Free Press, 1949). The quotations from Blumenbach and Montaigne (**18**) are in Peter Wood, "Race," in *Encyclopedia of American Social History,* ed. Mary Kupiec Cayton et al. (New York: Charles Scribner's Sons, 1993), vol. I, 443 and 441; Ashley Montagu is quoted (**19**) on 437.

Paul Cuffe's remarkable life is revealed by Sheldon H. Harris, *Paul Cuffe, Black America, and the African Return* (New York: Simon and Schuster, 1972), and Lamont D. Thomas, *Paul Cuffe, Black Entrepreneur and Pan-Africanist* (Urbana: University of Illinois Press, 1988). The *Liverpool Mercury* compliment to Cuffe (**22**) is taken from Sidney Kaplan, *The Black Presence in the Era of the American Revolution* (Greenwich, CT: New York Graphic Society, 1973), 138.

THE MINGLING OF BLOOD ON NEW WORLD FRONTIERS

Theodore Roosevelt's stark language about the destiny of Europeans to kill Indians that opens this chapter (**23**) is from *The Winning of the West,* in *The Works of Theodore Roosevelt,* vol. XI (New York: Charles Scribner's Sons, 1924), 274–75. A scholarly book on his racial thinking is Thomas G. Dyer, *Theodore Roosevelt and the Idea of Race* (Baton Rouge: Louisiana State University Press, 1980). A lively and perceptive biography is Henry F. Pringle, *Theodore Roosevelt* (San Diego: Harcourt Brace Jovanovich, 1984).

For two studies of racial interaction in early America, see Gary B. Nash, *Red, White, and Black: The Peoples of Early North America,* 4th ed. (Englewood Cliffs, NJ: Prentice Hall, 1999), and Colin Calloway, *New Worlds for All: Indians, Europeans, and the Remaking of Early America* (Baltimore: Johns Hopkins University Press, 1997).

The comments on Black Prince, the Iroquois leader (**26**), are recorded in Witham Marshe, *Lancaster in 1744: Journal of the Treaty at Lancaster in 1744, with the Six Nations,* ed. William H. Egle (Lancaster, PA: New Era Steam and Job Print, 1884), 12. Interracial marriages among fur traders (**27**) are perceptively discussed by John Mack Faragher, "The Custom of the Country: Cross-Cultural Marriage in the Far Western Fur Trade," in *Western Women: Their Land, Their Lives,* ed. Lillian Schlissel, Vicki L. Ruiz, and Janice Monk (Albuquerque: University of New Mexico Press, 1988), 199–215; Michael Laframbois's boast (**28**) is in this essay, 201.

For spirited biographies of Jim Bridger and Kit Carson, see Gene Caesar, *King of the Mountain Men: The Life of Jim Bridger* (New York: Dutton, 1961); Stanley Vestal, *Jim Bridger, Mountain Man* (Lincoln: University of Nebraska Press, 1946); and Thelma S. Guild and Harvey L. Carter, *Kit Carson: A Pattern for Heroes* (Lincoln: University of Nebraska Press, 1984). The John Lawson quotation (**30**) is from Hugh T. Lefler, ed., *A New Voyage to Carolina by John Lawson* (Chapel Hill: University of North Carolina Press, 1967), 189–90. For Huron and Ottawa women's preferences (**30**), see Jacqueline Peterson, "Women Dreaming: The Religiopsychology of Indian-White Marriages," in Jacqueline Peterson and Jennifer S. H. Brown, eds., *The New Peoples: Being and Becoming Metis in North America* (Winnipeg: University of Manitoba Press, 1985), 54.

The lives of William Johnson, Degonwadonti (Molly Brant), and Joseph Brant are chronicled in James T. Flexner's fast-paced *Lord of the Mohawks* (Boston: Little, Brown, 1979) and in Isabel Thompson Kelsay's *Joseph Brant, 1743–1807: Man of Two Worlds* (Syracuse, NY: Syracuse University Press, 1984). The quote on Johnson's affinity for Iroquois people (**30**) is from Calloway, *New Worlds for All,* 154.

Narratives about Indian captivity have fascinated Americans for three centuries. A historical novel of a white woman who was transformed by her Indian captivity experience is James Alexander Thom's *The Red Heart* (New York: Ballantine Books, 1997). James Axtell has much to say about how white captives refused to return home in "The White Indians of Colonial America," in *The European and the Indian* (New York: Oxford University Press, 1981). For the remarkable life story of Eunice Williams, see John Demos, *The Unredeemed Captive: A Family Story from Early America* (New York: Alfred A. Knopf, 1994); the sermon on "made of one blood" (**37**) is quoted on 247 and 252.

For learning more about French-Indian cultural interaction, see the interesting essays in Peterson and Brown, *The New Peoples*. Colbert's directive urging racial intermarriage (**38**) is quoted in Nash, *Red, White, and Black,* 106.

New Orleans, and Louisiana in general, is a unique case of racial mixing in the United States. For a scholarly treatment of this, see Virginia Dominguez, *White by Definition: Social Classification in Creole Louisiana* (New Brunswick, NJ: Rutgers University Press, 1986). The comment on the thoroughly intermixed society of early New Orleans (**38–39**) is from Joel Williamson, *New People: Miscegenation and Mulattoes in the United States* (New York: Free Press, 1980), 20–21.

Black-Indian intermarriage can be explored in Kenneth W. Porter, *The Negro on the American Frontier* (New York: Arno Press, 1971). Two more difficult books but ones filled with insights are Jack Forbes, *Black Africans and Native Americans: Color, Race, and Class in the Evolution of Red-Black People* (Oxford: Blackwell, 1988), and Theda Perdue, *Slavery and the Evolution of Cherokee Society, 1540–1866* (Knoxville: University of Tennessee Press, 1979). The creation of tri-racial communities along the eastern seaboard is followed in Brewton Berry's accessible *Almost White: A Study of Certain Racial Hybrids in the Eastern United States* (New York: Macmillan, 1963). For those wanting a more specialized study, see Karen I. Blu, *The Lumbee Problem: The Making of an American Indian People* (New York: Cambridge University Press, 1980). One fascinating group of African-Americans who became Indianized without mingling their blood with Native Americans is studied by Kevin Mulroy, *Freedom on the Border: The Seminole Maroons in Florida, the Indian Territory, Coahuila, and Texas* (Lubbock: Texas Tech University Press, 1993).

For the power of the Iroquois (**41**), see Nash, *Red, White, and Black,* 227. Jefferson's approval of white-Indian mixing (**43**) is recorded in a brash book by Richard Drinnon, *Facing West: The Metaphysics of Indian-Hating and Empire-Building* (Minneapolis: University of Minnesota Press, 1980), 83. Jefferson told the world about his views of the inferiority of Africans and the need to separate white and black Americans in his *Notes on the State of Virginia,* first published in Paris in 1785. A modern edition with an introduction by Thomas P. Abernethy is *Thomas Jefferson's Notes on the State of Virginia* (New York: Harper & Row, 1964); the quotes from Jefferson (**43**) are in this book, 139, and in John Miller, *The Wolf by the Ears: Thomas Jefferson and Slavery* (New York: Free Press, 1977), 278.

Mary Musgrove's life can be followed in Michele Gillespie, "The Sexual Politics of Race and Gender: Mary Musgrove and the Georgia Trustees," in *The Devil's*

Lane: Sex and Race in the Early South, ed. Catherine Clinton and Michele Gillespie (New York: Oxford University Press, 1997), 187–204.

RACE IN THE AMERICAS: THE SPANISH AND ENGLISH DIFFERENCE

For comparisons between English and Spanish colonizers in their sexual relations with Africans and Native Americans, see Nash, *Red, White, and Black,* especially chapter 12 on "The Mixing of People"; Magnus Morner, *Race Mixture in the History of Latin America* (Boston: Little, Brown, 1967); and Marvin Harris, *Patterns of Race in the Americas* (New York: Walker, 1964).

Winthrop D. Jordan's *White over Black: American Attitudes Toward the Negro, 1550–1812* (Chapel Hill: University of North Carolina Press, 1968) is a huge, brilliant book that must be digested slowly; for those with smaller appetites a compressed version is available: *The White Man's Burden: Historical Origins of Racism in the United States* (New York: Oxford University Press, 1974). No historian has delved deeper into white people's racial attitudes in early American history or into early black-white relations.

Two beautifully illustrated books with insightful essays that explore the *casta* paintings are Maria Concepcion Garcia Saiz, *Las castas Méxicanas: Un género pictorico americano* (Milan: Olivetti, 1989), which has parallel Spanish and English essays and captions, and *New World Orders: Casta Painting and Colonial Latin America* (New York: Americas Society Art Gallery, 1996). The quotation about gene pools (**49**) is from Jorge Klor de Alva, "*Mestizaje* from New Spain to Aztlan: On the Control and Classification of Collective Identities" and can be found in the latter book, 60. The comment from the German visitor, Alexander von Humboldt, to Mexico (**58**) is from Ilona Katzew, "Casta Painting: Identity and Social Stratification in Colonial Mexico," in *New World Orders,* 9. The observation about Spanish blood wiping away the stain of Indianness (**58**) is from the same book, 11.

THE UNITED STATES OF THE DISUNITED RACES

Black-white racial blending in the era of slavery is discussed in the following broad studies: Albert Murray, *The Omni-Americans: New Perspectives on Black Experience and American Culture* (New York: Outerbridge and Dienstfrey, 1970); and Joel Williamson, *New People: Miscegenation and Mulattoes in the United States* (New York: Free Press, 1980). For Indian-white blending, a number of rewarding essays on particular figures are found in Margaret Connell Szasz, ed., *Between Indian and White Worlds: The Cultural Broker* (Norman: University of Oklahoma Press,

1994); and Frances Karttunen, *Between Worlds: Interpreters, Guides and Survivors* (New Brunswick, NJ: Rutgers University Press, 1994).

The dream of T.T. (**65–66**) was published in William Lloyd Garrison's fiery abolitionist newspaper *The Liberator* on April 2, 1831; the reaction of blacks (**66**) was in the April 30 issue. Tom Paine's queries about American happiness (**67–68**) can be found in Philip S. Foner, ed., *The Complete Writings of Thomas Paine*, vol. II (New York: Citadel Press, 1945), 82; and Nelson F. Adkins, ed., *Common Sense and Other Political Writings* (Indianapolis: Bobbs-Merrill, 1953), 51.

The question and prediction about American people (**68**) is from J. Hector Saint John de Crèvecoeur, *Letters from an American Farmer* (1782; New York: E. P. Dutton & Company, 1912), 43.

The soaring language in the preamble of Pennsylvania's abolition law of 1780 (**68**), representing the height of Enlightenment thought in revolutionary America, is available in Roger Bruns, *Am I Not a Man and a Brother: The Antislavery Crusade of Revolutionary America, 1688–1788* (New York: Chelsea House, 1977), 446. Thomas Fuller (**69**) is described in Jordan, *White over Black*, 449. For the career of Benjamin Banneker (**69, 71**), see Silvio A. Bedini, *The Life of Benjamin Banneker* (Rancho Cordova, CA: Landmark Enterprises, 1972); the essay on Banneker, by James McHenry, appeared first in the Philadelphia *General Advertizer,* Dec. 28, 1790. For Belknap's opinion (**71**), see Jordan, *White over Black*, 457. Banneker's letter to Jefferson (**71**) is in Sidney Kaplan, *The Black Presence in the Era of the American Revolution* (Greenwich, CT: New York Graphic Society, 1973), 118–19. The New York law (**71**) is quoted in Jordan, *White over Black,* 470–71. Dumas Malone is Jefferson's biographer who found the affair with Hemings unthinkable (**72**) in *Jefferson the President, First Term, 1801–1805* (Boston: Little, Brown, 1970). The Virginia legislator's worry about racial intermixing (**72**) is quoted in Jordan, *White over Black,* 580–81.

For the hardening of racial attitudes in Philadelphia, see Gary B. Nash, *Forging Freedom: The Formation of Philadelphia's Black Community, 1720–1840* (Cambridge: Harvard University Press, 1989); the minister at Old Swedes Church and the Methodist (**73**) are quoted in this book (with spellings as originally used), 180. A broad-ranging book on hardening white racial attitudes in the nineteenth century is George Fredrickson, *The Black Image in the White Mind: The Debate on Afro-American Character and Destiny, 1817–1914* (Middletown, CT: Wesleyan University Press, 1971).

Jefferson made his gloomy comments about American Indians to Baron von Humboldt, Dec. 6, 1813 (**73**); the letter is in *Writings of Jefferson,* vol. XIV, 23. Tench Coxe's ominous views (**74**) were set forth in his "Considerations Respecting the Helots of the United States, African and Indian, Native and Alien, and Their

Descendants of the Whole and Mixed Blood" in the Philadelphia newspaper *Democratic Press*, Nov. 25, 1820–Feb. 5, 1821, quoted in Nash, *Forging Freedom,* 225.

Samuel George Morton is aptly described in William Stanton's *The Leopard's Spots: Scientific Attitudes Toward Race in America, 1815–1859* (Chicago: University of Chicago Press, 1960); the quoted passage about Morton (**76**) is on 27. Morton's conclusions about racial capabilities (**76**) are quoted in Sven Lindqvist, *The Skull Measurer's Mistake* (New York: The New Press, 1995), 43. For a good account of Josiah Nott (**77**), see Reginald Horsman, *Race and Manifest Destiny: The Origins of American Racial Anglo-Saxonism* (Cambridge: Harvard University Press, 1981), 130. The frenzy over measuring skulls as a test of character is explored in John D. Davies, *Phrenology: Fad and Science, A Nineteenth-Century American Crusade* (New Haven: Yale University Press, 1955). Washington Irving's views on racial gradations (**77**) are quoted in Eric Sundquist, *Cambridge History of American Literature,* vol. II (Cambridge: Cambridge University Press, 1995), 138–39. John Quincy Adams (**77**) is quoted in Alexander Saxton, *The Rise and Fall of the White Republic: Class, Politics, and Mass Culture in Nineteenth-Century America* (London: Verso Press, 1990), 89. For George Lippard (**78**), see Sundquist, *History of American Literature,* 161.

The first racist cartoonists are discussed in Nash, *Forging Freedom,* 254–59. The complaint of the free black leader in Boston (**78**) is in Hosea Easton, *A Treatise on the Intellectual Character and Civil and Political Condition of the Colored People of the United States and the Prejudice Exercised Against Them* (1837; Philadelphia: Rhistoric Publications, 1969), 42. For the nineteenth-century fascination with minstrelsy, see Robert C. Toll, *Blacking Up: The Minstrel Show in Nineteenth-Century America* (New York: Oxford University Press, 1984). Two more difficult but important books are David R. Roediger, *The Wages of Whiteness: Race and the Making of the American Working Class* (London: Verso, 1991); and Eric Lott, *Love and Theft: Blackface Minstrelsy and the American Working Class* (New York: Oxford University Press, 1993). The quotation on the appetite of white northerners for minstrel shows (**82**) is from Toll's "Minstrels/Minstrelsy," in *Encyclopedia of African-American Culture and History,* ed. Jack Salzman, David Lionel Smith, and Cornel West, vol. IV (New York: Macmillan, 1995), 1811.

The story of Nathan Sayre and his mixed-race family is told in Adele Logan, *Ambiguous Lives: Free Women of Color in Rural Georgia, 1789–1879* (Fayetteville: University of Arkansas Press, 1991). The life of Richard Mentor Johnson with his black mistress, in effect a common-law wife, is recounted in Leland W. Meyer, *The Life and Times of Colonel Richard Mentor Johnson of Kentucky* (New York: Columbia University Press, 1932). For information about Judge John Hemphill, I am indebted to James Paulsen, South Texas College of Law.

For a fine biography of the fascinating William Lloyd Garrison, see John L. Thomas, *The Liberator: William Lloyd Garrison* (Boston: Little, Brown, 1963). The quote from Garrison (**85**) is from *The Liberator*, April 2, 1831. Garrison's comment about black skin becoming popular (**85**) is from Walter M. Merrill and Louis Ruchames, eds., *Letters of William Lloyd Garrison*, 6 vols. (Cambridge: Harvard University Press, 1971–1981), vol. I, 128. Garrison's quip about graduating love by feet and inches and his opinion that black Americans were rarely interested in racial intermarriage (**85**) is from *The Liberator*, May 21, 1831. For an account of the squabble over interracial marriage in Garrison's Massachusetts, see Louis Ruchames, "Race, Marriage, and Abolition in Massachusetts," *Journal of Negro History* 40 (1955): 250–73. The quotation from David Ruggles (**85**) is given in James Horton and Lois Horton, *Free People of Color: Inside the African American Community* (Washington, DC: Smithsonian Institution Press, 1993), 143. The other quotation from the reformer about obstructing "the flow of affections" (**85–86**) is from *The Liberator*, May 7, 1831. The final quote in this paragraph (**86**) is from Mary Frances Berry and John W. Blassingame, *Long Memory: The Black Experience in America* (New York: Oxford University Press, 1982), 131.

The two excerpts from Herman Melville (**86**) are from *Redburn: His First Voyage, Being the Sailor-Boy Confessions and Reminiscences of the Son-of-a-Gentleman, in the Merchant Service* (1849; Evanston, IL: Northwestern University Press, 1969), 169; and *The Confidence Man: His Masquerade* (1857; New York: Hendricks House, 1954), 216.

Ralph Waldo Emerson's long literary career is movingly described by Robert D. Richardson, *Emerson: The Mind on Fire* (Berkeley and Los Angeles: University of California Press, 1995). The quotation from Emerson (**86**) is from *Emerson in His Journals*, ed. Joel Porte (Cambridge: Harvard University Press, 1982), 347. Wendell Phillips's memorable plea for the "United States of the United Races" (**86–87**) was published in *National Era* VII (September 1853); his other quote about "harmonious and equal mingling of all races" is in Gilbert Osofsky, "Wendell Phillips and the Quest for a New American Identity," *Canadian Review of Studies in Nationalism* I (Fall 1973): 37–39. For a spirited biography of Phillips, see Irving Bartlett, *Wendell Phillips: Brahmin Radical* (Boston: Beacon Press, 1961).

John Russwurm's life can be reviewed in James Wesley Smith, *Sojourners in Search of Freedom: The Settlement of Liberia by Black Americans* (Lanham, MD: University Press of America, 1987). The life of William Apess is told in Bernd C. Peyer, *The Tutor'd Mind: Indian Missionary-Writers in Antebellum America* (Amherst: University of Massachusetts Press, 1997), 117–65.

Cherokee and Choctaw cross-cultural marriages can be followed in Rachel C. Easton, *John Ross and the Cherokee Indians* (New York: AMS Press, 1978), and Benjamin W. Griffith, Jr., *McIntosh and Weatherford, Creek Indian Leaders* (Tuscaloosa: University of Alabama Press, 1988). Stand Watie's story is told in Frank Cunningham, *General Stand Watie's Confederate Indians* (San Antonio: Naylor, 1959); Ely Parker's life is related in William H. Armstrong, *Ely S. Parker: Union General and Seneca Chief* (Syracuse, NY: Syracuse University Press, 1978).

Lemuel Haynes has found his biographer in John Saillant, "Lemuel Haynes's Black Republicanism and the American Republican Tradition, 1775–1820," *Journal of the Early Republic* XIV (1994): 293–324. The memorial celebrating his accomplishments (**91**) was given by Timothy Mather Cooley, *Sketches of the Life and Character of the Rev. Lemuel Haynes* (New York: J. S. Taylor, 1839).

BUILDING WALLS

The Civil War has long been more popular to read about than Reconstruction, but the two were joined at the hip and ought to be considered together. An eye-opening book for young readers, filled with absorbing primary documents, is William Friedheim, *Freedom's Unfinished Revolution: An Inquiry into the Civil War and Reconstruction* (New York: The New Press, 1996). More scholarly and wide reaching on the Freedmen's Bureau and Reconstruction is Eric Foner, *Reconstruction: America's Unfinished Revolution, 1863–1877* (New York: Harper & Row, 1988).

The "Black Republican Prayer" and the "United Matrimonial Paint Shop" excerpts (**92, 93**) are taken from Sidney Kaplan, "The Miscegenation Issue in the Election of 1864," *Journal of Negro History* 34 (1949): 276 and 325. An excellent treatment of how the Democratic Party played the race card is Forrest G. Wood, *Black Scare: The Racist Response to Emancipation and Reconstruction* (Berkeley and Los Angeles: University of California Press, 1968). Martha Hodes draws back the curtain on a forbidden chapter of American southern history in *White Women, Black Men: Illicit Sex in the Nineteenth-Century South* (New Haven, CT: Yale University Press, 1997). Social Darwinism is an important topic in the history of American race relations. It can be explored in Carl Degler's *In Search of Human Nature: The Decline and Revival of Darwinism in American Social Thought* (New York: Oxford University Press, 1991). The "first step backwards" comment by Josiah Royce (**97**) is quoted in Thomas F. Gossett, *Race: The History of an Idea in America* (New York: Schocken Books, 1965), 67, as is the opinion of the northern Congregational minister, Asa Gray. The white South Carolinian's opinion on the doomed Negro race and Hinton Helper's diatribe about Negro degeneracy (**97, 98**) are also from Gossett, *Race,* 256, 262–63.

Gossett provides a useful introduction to the southern race extremists. The excerpts on Senator Ben Tillman and Governor James Vardaman (**99**) are quoted in *Race,* 171. For the Thomas Nelson Page excerpt (**99**), see *The Negro: The Southerner's Problem* (New York: Charles Scribner's Sons, 1904), 80, 163.

The excerpt (**99**) from Thomas Dixon's book, *The Clansman: An Historical Romance of the Ku Klux Klan* (New York: Grosset & Dunlap, 1905), is on 57–58. For a full account of D. W. Griffith's movie, *Birth of a Nation,* and its enormous impact on the country, see Richard Schickel, *D. W. Griffith: An American Life* (New York: Simon and Schuster, 1984). The quotes from Frederick Douglass and Ida Barnett Wells (**101**) are taken from Martha Hodes, "The Sexualization of Reconstruction Politics: White Women and Black Men in the South After the Civil War," in John C. Fout and Maura S. Tantillo, *American Sexual Politics: Sex, Gender, and Race Since the Civil War* (Chicago: University of Chicago Press, 1993), 73. For laws prohibiting interracial marriage, see David Fowler, *Northern Attitudes Towards Interracial Marriage, 1780–1930* (New York: Garland Publishers, 1987). Paul R. Spickard's *Mixed Blood: Intermarriage and Ethnic Identity in Twentieth-Century America* (Madison: University of Wisconsin Press, 1989), a key book for studying interreligious, interethnic, and interracial marriage in the twentieth century, provides a useful table of state legislation banning intermarriage. Also useful is Williamson, *New People,* from which the statement by Julian Bond's father (**104**) is taken, 109. A fascinating study on the difficulties of the courts to find acceptable definitions of race and racial categories—but a book for the advanced reader—is Ian Haney-Lopez, *White by Law: The Legal Construction of Race* (New York: New York University Press, 1996).

E. Franklin Frazier's study of African-American society in the early twentieth century is *The Negro Family in the United States* (Chicago: University of Chicago Press, 1932). On hair relaxers and bleaching creams, see Jervis Anderson, *This Was Harlem* (New York: Farrar, Straus and Giroux, 1982). The data on "passing" (**106–7**) is from Spickard, *Mixed Blood,* 336.

The hostility to Asian immigrants on the West Coast is the theme of Alexander Saxton's important and scholarly book *The Indispensable Enemy: Labor and the Anti-Chinese Movement in California* (Berkeley and Los Angeles: University of California Press, 1971). A broader treatment of white racism in California is Tomás Almaguer, *Racial Fault Lines: The Historical Origins of White Supremacy in California* (Berkeley and Los Angeles: University of California Press, 1994). Henry George (**107**) is quoted in Saxton, *Indispensable Enemy,* 102. For Hinton Helper's racist comments (**107**), see Gossett, *Race,* 262. The delegate at California's Constitutional Convention in 1878 (**107**) is quoted in Ronald Takaki, *A Different Mirror: A History of Multicultural America* (Boston: Little, Brown, 1993), 205. For the AFT quote about coolies (**109**), see Saxton, *Indispensable Enemy,* 271; the petition to Congress (**109**) is quoted on 272.

The eugenics movement is covered ably in Gossett, *Race,* and in George Fredrickson, *The Arrogance of Race: Historical Perspectives on Slavery, Racism, and Social Inequality* (Middletown, CT: Wesleyan University Press, 1988). A more difficult book, though very valuable, is Daniel J. Kevles, *In the Name of Eugenics: Genetics and the Uses of Human Heredity* (New York: Alfred A. Knopf, 1985). Madison Grant (**110**) is quoted from his *Passing of the Great Race* (1916; New York: Charles Scribner's Sons, 1921), 17–18, 45–47, and 228. The temper of the times can be measured in another race purity tract: Theodore Lothrop Stoddard, *The Rising Tide of Color Against White World-Supremacy* (New York: Charles Scribner's Sons, 1920). The growing hostility toward Eastern and Southern European immigrants can be explored further in John Higham, *Strangers in the Land: Patterns of American Nativism, 1860–1925* (New Brunswick, NJ: Rutgers University Press, 1955). The particularly virulent hostility to Jews can be followed in Spickard, *Mixed Blood,* chapter six; the quote (**111**) is from Spickard, *Mixed Blood,* 182.

Edmonia Lewis's life has never been fully studied, but useful short essays are Stephen May, "The Object at Hand," *Smithsonian Magazine* (Sept. 1996): 16–19; and Marilyn Richardson, "Edmonia Lewis," in *Encyclopedia of African-American Culture and History,* vol. III, 1607–08. The quotation about Lewis's *Death of Cleopatra* (**113**) appeared in *The People's Advocate,* an Alexandria, Virginia, newspaper (May 1876): 19.

INTERRACIAL RENEGADES

The incredible Healy family saga is well told in Albert Foley, *Bishop Healy: Beloved Outcaste* (New York: Farrar, Straus, and Young, 1954); Foley, *God's Men of Color: The Colored Catholic Priests of the United States, 1854–1954* (New York: Farrar, Straus, and Young, 1955); and *Dream of an Outcaste: Patrick F. Healy* (Tuscaloosa: Portals Press, 1976). The New York newspaper comment on Captain Michael Healy (**117**) is from the fine article by James M. O'Toole, "Racial Identity and the Case of Captain Michael Healy, USRCS," *Prologue* 29 (1997): 198.

The sad case of Elizabeth Hulme is taken from *New York Times,* March 13, 1885. I am grateful to Joan Waugh, UCLA, for calling this case to my attention.

Lucy Parsons's biographer, Caroline Ashbaugh, provides a lively account of her remarkable life in *Lucy Parsons: American Revolutionary* (Chicago: Charles H. Kerr, 1976); the quote from William Parsons (**120**) is on page 13 of this book.

Tye Leung and Charles Schulze (**124**) are chronicled in Judy Yung, *Unbound Feet: A Social History of Chinese Women in San Francisco* (Berkeley and Los Angeles: University of California Press, 1995), 170–73. A wonderful biography of Frederick Douglass is William S. McFeely, *Frederick Douglass* (New York: Simon and Schuster, 1991); but even better than a biography is Douglass's autobiography, one of the finest books of its kind in American history. See *Narrative of the Life of Frederick Douglass: An American Slave, Written by Himself,* ed. Benjamin Quarles (1849; Cambridge: Harvard University Press, 1988). The quotation about Douglass's appeal (**124**) is from Fredrickson, *Arrogance of Race,* 81.

The controversial Jack Johnson, always exciting to read about, can be explored in two biographies: Al-Tony Gilmore, *Bad Nigger! The National Impact of Jack Johnson* (Port Washington, NY: Kennikat Press, 1975); and Randy Roberts, *Papa Jack: Jack Johnson and the Era of White Hopes* (New York: Free Press, 1983). The newspaper report of Johnson's victory over Jeffries (**126**) is quoted from Lawrence W. Levine, *Black Culture and Black Consciousness: Afro-American Folk Thought from Slavery to Freedom* (New York: Oxford University Press, 1977), 431.

For Oberlin and Oneida colleges see Robert Samuel Fletcher, *A History of Oberlin College From Its Foundation Through the Civil War,* 2 vols. (Oberlin, OH: Oberlin College, 1943); and Milton C. Sernett, *Abolition's Axe: Beriah Green, Oneida Institute, and the Black Freedom Struggle* (Syracuse, NY: Syracuse University Press, 1986). "Will be blown sky high" (**127**) is from Fletcher, vol. 2, 523; "a motley company" (**128**) is from Sernett, 51; "the red sons" (**128**) is also in Sernett, 63.

The Old West of dime novels and Hollywood movies has come in for a thorough revamping at the hands of new historians. Ramón A. Gutiérrez provides a compelling picture of ethnic crossings in the Spanish Southwest in *When Jesus Came, the Corn Mothers Went Away: Marriage, Sexuality, and Power in New Mexico, 1500–1846* (Stanford: Stanford University Press, 1991). The thoroughly mixed-race character of the West after it became American territory in 1848 is illuminated by Patricia Nelson Limerick in *The Legacy of Conquest: The Unbroken Past of the American West* (New York: W. W. Norton and Co., 1987). For "we are building a nation" (**127**), see William Barrows, "The Half-Breed Indians of North America," *Andover Review* 12 (1889): 35–36. A beautiful book of illustrations with fine essays is *The West: An Illustrated History* (Boston: Little, Brown, 1996).

The Punjabi-Mexican crossing in California is fully documented in Karen I. Leonard, *Making Ethnic Choices: California's Punjabi Mexican Americans* (Philadelphia: Temple University Press, 1992). "Cotton was the crop" (**129**) appears on page 63 of this book. For another mixed-race community on the East Coast, see Marilyn Halter, *Between Race and Ethnicity: Cape Verdean American Immigrants, 1860–1965* (Urbana: University of Illinois Press, 1993).

TEARING WALLS DOWN

The story of Emma Ellen Howse and Walter Ngong Fong is taken from a series of autobiographical articles published in the *San Francisco Bulletin* from May 29 to June 12, 1922, and the news reports of her marriage in the *San Francisco Chronicle,* June 20, 1897, and the *Rocky Mountain News,* June 20, 1897. I am grateful to Henry Yu, UCLA, for copies of these materials. The *San Francisco Bulletin* editorial (**133**) is from the June 15, 1922, edition. The rise of the KKK can be followed in Kenneth T. Jackson, *The Ku Klux Klan in the City, 1915–1930* (New York: Oxford University Press, 1967); and William Loren Katz's more popular treatment, *The Invisible Empire* (Washington, DC: Open Hand Publishers, 1986). The quotation from Kenneth Roberts (**133**) is from Gossett, *Race,* 402.

Chicago in the era of jazz and the blues is presented in William H. Kenney, *Chicago Jazz: A Cultural History* (New York: Oxford University Press, 1993); Marshall Stearns, *The Story of Jazz* (New York: Oxford University Press, 1956); Paul Oliver, *The Story of the Blues* (Philadelphia: Chilton, 1969); and Amiri Baraka [LeRoi Jones], *Blues People: The Negro Experience in White America and the Music That Developed from It* (New York: William Morrow, 1963). For "teenage refugees from the sunny suburbs" (**134**) and jazz "as a new religion" (**134**), see Levine, *Black Culture and Black Consciousness,* 295 and 294. The University of Chicago's cutting-edge academics are explored in Henry Yu, "Thinking About Orientals: Modernity, Social Science, and Asians in Twentieth-Century America" (Ph.D. diss., Princeton University, 1995), 39–143; and Winifred Raushenbush, *Robert E. Park: Biography of a Sociologist* (Durham, NC: Duke University Press, 1979). The survey questions about racial intermarriage (**136**) are from *Orientals and Their Cultural Adjustment* (Nashville: Social Science Institute, Fisk University, 1946). For José Vasconcelos's lectures on hybridism (**136**), see "The Race Problem in Latin America," in Vasconcelos, *Aspects of Mexican Civilization* (Chicago: University of Chicago Press, 1926), 85; and (**137**) Vasconcelos, *The Cosmic Race/La Raza Cosmica: A Bilingual Edition* (1925; Los Angeles: Centro de Publicaciones, 1979), 18.

Among the many books on the Harlem Renaissance and the Greenwich Village of the 1920s, the most accessible are David Levering Lewis, *When Harlem Was in Vogue* (New York: Alfred A. Knopf, 1981); and Ann Douglass, *Terrible Honesty: Mongrel Manhattan in the 1920s* (New York: Farrar, Straus and Giroux, 1995). For

E. A. Ross's observations on immigrants (**137, 139**), see Gossett, *Race,* 293. Randolph Bourne is best understood by reading his essays, published in *War and the Intellectuals: Essays, 1915–1919,* ed. Carl Resek (New York: Harper and Row, 1964); the quote from Bourne (**139**) is on 121. For Boas's comment on "the greatest hope" (**140**) see Degler, *In Search of Human Nature,* 79.

A biography exists for almost every figure of the Harlem Renaissance; the biography of Langston Hughes by Arnold Rampersad, *The Life of Langston Hughes,* 2 vols. (New York: Oxford University Press, 1986–1988), puts the reader in touch with the entire cast of poets, patrons, artists, musicians, dancers, novelists, journalists, and impresarios. For "this cosmopolitan city" (**142**), see Douglas, *Mongrel Manhattan,* 385.

For black American emigrés in France and their cosmopolitan, often interracial, experience there, see Tyler Stovall, *Paris Noir: African Americans in the City of Light* (Boston: Houghton Mifflin, 1996). On interracial love and marriage in the Harlem Renaissance, see Douglas, *Mongrel Manhattan,* chapter seven: "Black Man and White Ladyship." Josephine Schuyler's comment on her Texas background (**144**) is in Schuyler, "Does Interracial Marriage Succeed?" in Clotye M. Larsson, *Marriage Across the Color Line* (Chicago: Johnson Publishing Co., 1965), 167. The Scottsboro Boys debacle is dissected in Dan T. Carter, *Scottsboro: A Tragedy of the American South* (New York: Pantheon, 1994). The quote about "their own faces and features accurately and lovingly reflected" (**145**) is from *The Norton Anthology of African American Literature,* ed. Henry Louis Gates, Jr., and Nelly Y. McKay (New York: W. W. Norton, 1997), 936.

The Depression and the attempts of the CIO to bring black and white workers together is covered well in Joshua Freeman, et al., *Who Built America? Working People and the Nation's Economy, Politics, Culture, and Society,* vol. 2 (New York: Pantheon, 1992); the Chicago worker's words (**146**) are on 408. Eleanor Roosevelt's crusade for racial justice is movingly explored in Doris Kearns Goodwin, *No Ordinary Time: Franklin and Eleanor Roosevelt: The Home Front in World War II* (New York: Simon and Schuster, 1994); "It is incomprehensible" (**147**), "We have not had a Negro working in 25 years" (**148**), "A bunch of snoopers" (**148**), and "I just couldn't do it" (**148**) are from this book, 172, 246–47, 370.

The story of Frances Fitzpatrick Osato is from the *San Francisco Examiner,* March 20, 1923. I am indebted to Henry Yu, UCLA, for this newspaper report.

RECAPTURING THE DREAM

The way *South Pacific* captured the American theater- and moviegoers is related in Stephen Citron, *The Wordsmiths: Oscar Hammerstein and Alan Jay Lerner* (New

York: Oxford University Press, 1995). The NAACP can be explored in Charles F. Kellogg, *NAACP: A History of the National Association for the Advancement of Colored People* (Baltimore: Johns Hopkins University Press, 1967). For "I'm comin' out a *man*" (**155**), see James T. Patterson, *Grand Expectations: The United States, 1945–1974* (New York: Oxford University Press, 1996), 23. The link between Hitler's Aryan race superiority complex and American racism (**155**) is analyzed in Stefan Kuhl, *The Nazi Connection: Eugenics, American Racism, and German National Socialism* (New York: Oxford University Press, 1994).

Eisenhower's comment "Every American should . . ." (**155**) is quoted in Patterson, *Grand Expectations*, 329; *Grand Expectations* is a fine introduction to the post–World War II decades. "The sixty-four-thousand-dollar question" (**156**) is from Poppy Cannon, *A Gentle Knight: My Husband, Walter White* (New York: Rinehart and Winston, 1956), 86. The significance of Jackie Robinson's career in professional baseball is told wonderfully in Jules Tygiel, *Baseball's Great Experiment: Jackie Robinson and His Legacy* (New York: Oxford University Press, 1983), and Arnold Rampersad, *Jackie Robinson* (New York: Alfred A. Knopf, 1997). The politics of early civil rights efforts is detailed in Patterson, *Grand Expectations*.

The battle in the courts over miscegenation laws is skillfully reconstructed by Peggy Pascoe, "Miscegenation Law, Court Cases, and Ideologies of 'Race' in Twentieth-Century America," *Journal of American History* 83 (1996): 44–69. For "What I am . . ." (**158**), see Spickard, *Mixed Blood*, 151; this book also documents the rapid increase in marriages between whites and Asian-Americans. For "I would prefer that [my children] marry a Japanese person" (**161**), see Valerie Matsumoto, *Farming the Home Place: A Japanese American Community in California, 1919–1982* (Ithaca, NY: Cornell University Press, 1993), 200. A good book on Japanese war brides is Evelyn Nakano Glenn, *Issei, Nisei, War Brides* (Philadelphia: Temple University Press, 1986); a poignant, personal account is in the play titled *Asa Ga Kimashita* (*Morning Has Broken*) by Velina Hasu Houston, who fell in love as a teenager with an African-American military policeman in occupied Japan after World War II. The play is published in Houston, ed., *The Politics of Life: Four Plays by Asian American Women* (Philadelphia: Temple University Press, 1993).

The interracial marriage of Walter White is told by his wife Poppy Cannon in *Gentle Knight*. For "I knew then who I was" (**161–2**), see Denton L. Watson, "Walter White," in *Encyclopedia of African American Culture and History*, vol. V, 2823. Other celebrity interracial marriages are noted in Spickard, *Mixed Blood*, 277–82, but the best way to explore what mixed-race couples experienced in America in this period is to read some of their autobiographies and biographies. Fast reads, for example, are Arnold Shaw, *Belafonte* (Philadelphia: Chilton, 1960); Lena Horne, *In Person: Lena Horne* (New York: Greenberg, 1950); Gail Lumet

Buckley, *The Hornes: An American Family* (New York: Knopf, 1986); Pearl Bailey, *Talking to Myself* (New York: Harcourt Brace Jovanovich, 1971); Katherine Dunham, *A Touch of Innocence* (New York: Harcourt Brace Jovanovich, 1959); and Sammy Davis, *Why Me? The Sammy Davis, Jr. Story* (New York: Farrar, Straus and Giroux, 1989).

The remarkable arrival of immigrants after Congress opened the doors to newcomers in 1965 is explored in Reed Ueda, *Postwar Immigrant America: A Social History* (Boston: Bedford Books, 1994). The landmark *Loving v. Virginia* case is analyzed in Pascoe, "Miscegenation Law," 64–68. The quotations (**164–5**) are from this article, 65–67. Garrison's moving advice on the pursuit of happiness (**165–6**) can be found in *The Liberator,* April 2, 1831.

Peggy Rusk's marriage to Guy Smith is reconstructed from Simeon Booker, "A Challenge for the Guy Smiths," *Ebony* 23 (1967): 146–50.

THE END OF WALLS?

Laurie Gantt's story (**169**) is related by Michael Frisby, "Black or Other?" *Emerge* (Dec.-Jan. 1996), 48–49. For the integration of the silver screen, a fascinating analysis is provided by Thomas Cripps, *Making Movies Black: The Hollywood Message Movie from World War II to the Civil Rights Era* (New York: Oxford University Press, 1993). For a breezier treatment, see James P. Murray, *To Find an Image: Black Films from Uncle Tom to Super Fly* (Indianapolis: Bobbs-Merrill, 1973).

The data on interracial marriages is drawn from Spickard, *Mixed Blood,* 306–7; Mark Nagler, "North American Indians and Intermarriage," in *Interracial Marriage: Expectations and Realities,* ed. Irving R. Stuart and Lawrence E. Abt (New York: Grossman Publishers, 1973); *New York Times* (December 2, 1991): A1, B6; Paul Ruffins, "Interracial Coalitions," *Atlantic* 265 (June 1990): 28–34; Robert E. T. Roberts, "Black-White Intermarriage in the United States," in Walton R. Johnson and D. Michael Warren, *Inside the Mixed Marriage: Accounts of Changing Attitudes, Patterns, and Perceptions of Cross-Cultural and Interracial Marriages* (Lanham, MD: University Press of America, 1994), 57–74; and various essays in Maria P. P. Root, *Racially Mixed People in America* (Newbury Park, CA: Sage Publications, 1992).

For "a sin against nature," "hybridism is heinous," and "mulattoes are monsters" (**173**), see the encyclopedic study, Werner Sollors, *Neither Black nor White Yet Both: Thematic Explorations of Interracial Literature* (New York: Oxford University Press, 1997), 298. Art Westinen (**173**) was quoted in the *Washington Post,* November 1, 1998.

The number of books on changes in racial consciousness, racial identity, and racial politics in the 1980s and 1990s grows weekly. Most are scholarly and will be difficult for young readers. Among the best are David G. Gutiérrez, *Walls and Mirrors: Mexican Americans, Mexican Immigrants, and the Politics of Identity* (Berkeley and Los Angeles: University of California Press, 1995); Peter Skerry, *Mexican Americans: The Ambivalent Minority* (New York: Free Press, 1993); Ronald Takaki, *A Different Mirror;* Paul R. Spickard, *Japanese Americans: The Formation and Transformations of an Ethnic Group* (New York: Twayne Publishers, 1996); John Higham, ed., *Civil Rights and Social Wrongs: Black-White Relations Since World War II* (University Park: Pennsylvania State University Press, 1997); Philip Gleason, *Speaking of Diversity: Language and Ethnicity in Twentieth-Century America* (Baltimore: Johns Hopkins University Press, 1992); Werner Sollors, ed., *Beyond Ethnicity* (New York: Oxford University Press, 1989); David A. Hollinger, *Postethnic America: Beyond Multiculturalism* (New York: Basic Books, 1995); Cornel West, *Race Matters* (Boston: Beacon Press, 1993); Mary C. Waters, *Ethnic Options: Choosing Identities in America* (Berkeley and Los Angeles: University of California Press, 1990), and William S. Penn, ed., *As We Are Now: Mixblood Essays on Race and Identity* (Berkeley and Los Angeles: University of California Press, 1998). For "I don't know what 'Hawaiian' is" (**176**), see Bernhard L. Horman, "Hawaii's Mixing People," in Noel P. Gist and Anthony Gary Dworkin, eds., *The Blending of Races: Marginality and Identity in World Perspective* (New York: Wiley-Interscience, 1972), 213.

For mixed-race clubs, see G. Reginald Daniel, "Beyond Black and White: The New Multiracial Consciousness," in Root, *Racially Mixed People in America,* 335; a survey of interracial clubs is G. Grosz, "From Sea to Shining Sea: A Current Listing of Interracial Organizations and Support Groups Across the Nation," *Interrace* 1 (1989): 24–28. The first class at Berkeley on racially mixed Americans (**178**) is related in *Los Angeles Times* (Jan. 9, 1996). The comments of Kaleena Crafton and Ramona Douglass (**179**) are from *Emerge* (Dec.-Jan. 1996): 49 and 54, and the statement of black leaders (**180**) is on 49–50. A thoughtful discussion of the debate over changing racial categories for the census in 2000 is Lawrence Wright, "One Drop of Blood," *New Yorker* (July 25, 1994): 46–55; the quote from Jon Michael Spender (**180**) is on 55. Itabari Njeri's *The Last Plantation: Color, Conflict, and Identity: Reflections of a New World Black* (Boston: Houghton Mifflin, 1997) has a penetrating analysis of this issue. For Cynthia Nakashima's comment (**180**), see *Los Angeles Times* (January 9, 1996). For "numbers drive the dollars" (**181**), see "Annals of Blood," 47.

The Wedowee, Alabama, incident, widely reported in newspapers and on television, can be followed in the *New York Times* (January 11, June 2, October 18, October 21, 1996).

By far the most empathetic way to explore interracial relationships in our own times is to read the autobiographies of those whose parents crossed the color line or who have themselves chosen spouses of a different race. Among the best are Itabari Njeri, *Every Good-Bye Ain't Gone: Family Portraits and Personal Escapades* (New York: Times Books, 1990); Imamu Amiri Baraka, *The Autobiography of LeRoi Jones* (Chicago: Lawrence Hill Books, 1997); Maya Angelou, *Singin' and Swingin' and Gettin' Merry Like Christmas* (New York: Random House, 1976); James McBride, *The Color of Water* (New York: Riverhead Books, 1996); Shirley Taylor Haizlip, *The Sweeter the Juice* (New York: Simon and Schuster, 1994); Mary Church Terrell, *A Colored Woman in a White World* (Washington, DC: National Association of Colored Women's Clubs, 1968). A scholarly collection of essays on racial intermarriage can be found in Walton R. Johnson and D. Michael Warren, eds., *Inside the Mixed Marriage: Accounts of Changing Attitudes, Patterns, and Perceptions of Cross-Cultural and Interracial Marriages* (Lanham, MD: University Press of America, 1994).

For Salman Rushdie's reflections on hybridism and his belief that "mongrelization" is the world's best hope, see his *Imaginary Homelands: Essays and Criticism, 1981–1991* (London: Granta Books, 1991); the quote (**183**) is on 394.

Index

(Page numbers in *italic* refer to illustrations.)